AGS

PRACTICAL GUIDE TO *B*ETTER ENGLISH

Level IV

Teacher's Guide

AGS®

American Guidance Service, Inc.
Circle Pines, Minnesota 55014-1796
1-800-328-2560

Printed in the United States of America

ISBN 0-7854-1799-0

Product Number 93081

A 0 9 8 7 6 5 4 3 2 1

CONTENTS

AGS *Practical Guide to Better English*

PROGRAM GOAL

The Practical Guide to Better English program is designed to help high school students and adults gain an awareness of the basic elements of the English language and develop proficiency in all the skills necessary for successful written communication in school and in the workplace.

OBJECTIVES

This new four-level program has the following objectives:

• Develop students' *mastery of essential grammar, usage, and mechanics skills* through focused instruction and practice.

• Build students' *vocabulary and store of background knowledge* through the use of informative, interesting real-world content.

• Improve students' *writing skills at the sentence, paragraph, and whole-composition levels* through the use of accessible models and directed practice in the various writing domains.

• Build students' *self-sufficiency in revising and proofreading* by providing a complete Handbook of grammar, usage, and mechanics rules bound into each pupil book. Students can use this as a resource when they revise written work in other classes and outside school.

Scope and Sequence of Grammar, Usage, and Mechanics Skills

	LEVEL		
	I	II	III	IV
CAPITALIZATION				
Capitalize first word in sentence	•	•	•	•
Capitalize proper nouns	•	•	•	•
Capitalize proper adjectives		•	•	•
Capitalize days of week		•	•	•
Capitalize months NOT seasons		•	•	•
Capitalize holidays, festivals		•	•	•
Capitalize the word *I*		•	•	•
CAPITALIZATION WITH PUNCTUATION				
Capitalize initial; use period		•	•	•
Capitalize personal title; use period		•	•	•
Capitalize abbreviations of day, week, month; use period		•	•	•
Capitals in addresses, punctuation		•	•	•
Commas in address in sentence		•	•	•
Capitalize words in titles		•	•	•
Draw line under title of book, movie		•	•	•
Quotation marks around title of poem, story		•	•	•
Direct vs. indirect quotations		•	•	•
Punctuate direct quotations		•	•	•
Commas in direct quotations		•	•	•
End punctuation in direct quotations		•	•	•
Quote inside quote: single quotation marks			•	•
OTHER USES OF COMMAS				
Comma in date (or no)	•	•	•	•
Comma after day, year	•	•	•	•
Comma after name, direct address	•	•	•	•
Comma after introductory word		•	•	•
Commas to set off interrupting word				•
Comma in compound sentence	•	•	•	•
Comma after introductory dependent clause		•	•	•
Commas to set off nonrestrictive clauses				•
Commas in series	•	•	•	•
Comma to separate adjectives				•
Appositive			•	•
Commas to set off appositive			•	•
PARTS OF SPEECH				
Nouns	•	•	•	•
Proper nouns	•	•	•	•
Nouns—singular and plural	•	•	•	•

	LEVEL		
	I	II	III	IV
Plural: most add -*s*	•	•	•	•
Plural with *ch, sh, s, x, z*	•	•	•	•
Plural with *f* or *fe*	•	•	•	•
Plural with consonant + *y*	•	•	•	•
Plural with vowel + *y*	•	•	•	•
Plurals: irregular		•	•	•
Some plurals same as singular		•	•	•
Possessive nouns			•	•
Possessive nouns: form singular with *'s*	•	•	•	•
Possessive nouns: plural ending in -*s* and NOT ending in -*s*	•	•	•	•
Pronouns: personal	•	•	•	•
Pronouns: subject	•	•	•	•
Pronouns: as direct object	•	•	•	•
Pronouns: object of preposition	•	•	•	•
Pronouns: *I* or *me* last in pair or series	•	•	•	•
Pronouns preceding nouns	•	•	•	•
Pronouns: compound personal	•	•	•	•
Pronouns: interrogative			•	•
Pronouns: demonstrative			•	•
Verbs: action, being	•	•	•	•
Verb phrase; helping verbs		•	•	•
Agreement in number	•	•	•	•
Agreement: *you are/were*	•	•	•	•
Agreement: *there is/are*	•	•	•	•
Agreement: compound subjects with *and/or*			•	•
Verbs: principal parts	•	•	•	•
First principal part		•	•	•
Second principal part			•	•
Third principal part			•	•
Present participle			•	•
Second and third principal parts sometimes the same			•	•
Simple verb tenses: past, present, future			•	•
Perfect tenses				•
Contractions	•	•	•	•
Adjectives	•	•	•	•
Articles (*an* before vowel)	•	•	•	•
Adjectives: demonstrative			•	•
Possessives act as adjectives			•	•
Use adjective (not adverb) as predicate adjective			•	•

Scope and Sequence of Grammar, Usage, and Mechanics Skills

	Level I	Level II	Level III	Level IV
Adjectives: comparative/superlative	•		•	•
Adverbs	•	•	•	•
Adverbs modify verbs	•	•	•	•
Adverbs modify adjectives			•	•
Adverbs modify adverbs			•	•
Don't confuse adverbs and adjectives				•
Adverbs: comparative/superlative			•	•
Prepositions	•	•	•	•
Prepositional phrases/elements		•	•	•
Prepositional phrases: adjectival			•	•
Prepositional phrases: adverbial			•	•
Prepositions: pairs with different meanings		•	•	•
Conjunctions: coordinating		•	•	•
Conjunctions: subordinating			•	•
Combining sentences	•	•	•	•
Interjections			•	•
VERBALS				
Verbals				•
Participle/participial phrase				•
Infinitive/infinitive phrase				•
Gerund/gerund phrase				•
TROUBLESOME VERBS				
Teach vs. *learn*	•	•	•	•
May vs. *can*	•	•	•	•
Sit vs. *set*	•	•	•	•
Lie (verb)			•	•
Lay (verb)			•	•
WORD STUDY				
Synonyms	•	•	•	•
Prepositional phrase used instead of a single word			•	•
Antonyms		•	•	•
Unnecessary words, eliminating	•	•	•	•
Negatives	•	•	•	•
Unsuitable expressions, eliminating	•	•	•	•
Homophones	•	•	•	•
SENTENCES				
Sentence/fragment/run-on/comma splice	•	•	•	•
Sentence: declarative	•	•	•	•
Sentence: interrogative	•	•	•	•

	Level I	Level II	Level III	Level IV
Sentence: imperative			•	•
Sentence: exclamatory	•	•	•	•
Subject/predicate—simple subject	•	•	•	•
Compound subject			•	•
Complete subject			•	•
Simple predicate	•		•	•
Compound predicate			•	•
Complete predicate			•	•
Subject or predicate, difficult to identify				•
Direct object/compound direct object			•	•
Indirect object				•
Object pronouns as indirect/direct objects		•	•	•
Predicate noun/predicate adjective		•	•	•
Simple sentence	•	•	•	•
Compound sentence	•	•	•	•
Complex sentence/dependent clause				•
Adjective clause				•
Adverb clause				•
PARAGRAPHS				
Paragraphs and compositions	•	•	•	•
Suggestions for writing a paragraph	•	•	•	•
LETTERS				
Friendly letter: parts	•	•	•	•
Friendly letter: capitalization/punctuation	•	•	•	
Business letter: parts	•	•	•	•
Business letter: greeting/close/signature			•	•
Business letter: capitalization/punctuation/postal codes	•		•	•
Envelope	•	•	•	•
USING A DICTIONARY				
Dictionary: introduction	•	•	•	•
Dictionary: alphabetical order	•	•	•	•
Syllables	•	•	•	•
Word division—introduction			•	•
Word division—rules			•	•
Respelling for pronunciation			•	•
Spelling	•	•	•	•
SPEAKING AND LISTENING				
Speaking	•	•	•	•
Listening	•	•	•	•

Student Book Organization

The *Practical Guide to Better English* **Student Book** for each level includes the following elements and features:

INSTRUCTION

- 72 one-page grammar/usage/mechanics *instructional lessons*—nine per unit.
- 8 two-page *composition lessons*—one per unit.
- 8 one-page grammar/usage/mechanics *unit reviews*—one per unit.

CUMULATIVE REVIEW

- A year-end review unit consisting of 9 one-page grammar/usage/ mechanics *review lessons* and a final two-page *cumulative review*.

HANDBOOK RESOURCE

- A *Handbook of grammar, usage, and mechanics rules* organized topically into 54 Guides.
- *Practice activities* following each Handbook section, for each principle explained in the Handbook.

Each lesson directs students to the appropriate Guide or Guides in the Handbook for explicit instruction in grammar, usage, and mechanics principles. In addition, an alphabetical index to topics covered in the Handbook is included at the end of the book.

WORD STUDY

- *Vocabulary puzzlers* of various kinds build students' knowledge of word structure, word meanings, and word relationships.

CORRELATION OF HANDBOOK GUIDES TO LESSONS

HANDBOOK GUIDE	LESSONS
1 Capitalization	8, 20, 31, 42, 53, 65, 79, 81, 87, 88, 97
Capitalization/Punctuation	
2 Initials of Names	8, 9, 65, 81, 87
3 Titles with Names	8, 16, 20, 65, 87, 97
4 Abbreviations	16, 78, 97
5 Addresses	16, 65, 79, 81, 87, 88, 97
6 Addresses in Sentences	9, 20, 31, 42, 53
7 Titles	42, 53, 97
8 Quotations	9, 20, 76
Other Uses of Commas	
9 Dates	9, 20, 31, 53, 65, 79, 87, 88, 97
10 Introductory/Interrupting Words	9, 16, 20, 22, 42
11 Compound Sentences/Dependent Clauses	12, 13, 15, 16, 20, 22, 42, 53, 89, 98
12 Items in Series	9, 16, 20, 31, 42, 53, 94
13 Appositives	16, 20, 22, 31, 42, 53
Parts of Speech	
14 Nouns	19, 23, 97
15 Singular & Plural Forms	18, 22, 95, 98
16 Possessive Forms	17, 18, 22, 42, 53, 95, 98
17 Pronouns	23, 24, 25, 26, 27, 28, 29, 30, 33, 76, 95, 98
18 Indefinite Pronouns	30
19 Interrogative Pronouns	30, 33
20 Demonstrative Pronouns	30
21 Verbs	37, 45
22 Verb Phrases	37, 45
23 Singular & Plural Forms	7, 46, 47, 52, 55, 63, 66, 74, 93, 96, 98
24 Principal Parts	3, 7, 48, 49, 50, 52, 55, 74, 84, 88, 96
25 Adjectives	10, 34, 36, 44, 74, 84, 96
26 Adverbs	10, 37, 38, 39, 44, 74, 84, 96
27 Prepositions	10, 24, 25, 40, 41, 44, 84, 96
28 Conjunctions	12, 13, 15, 22, 67, 69
29 Interjections	76, 83
30 Contractions	51, 55, 95
31 Verbals	56, 57, 58, 59, 60, 61, 66, 91, 98
Troublesome Verbs	
32 *Teach* and *Learn*	96
33 *May* and *Can*	84
34 *Sit* and *Set*	85, 88, 96
35 *Lie* and *Lay*	85, 88
Word Study	
36 Synonyms	62
37 Prepositional Phrases	40
38 Antonyms	62
39 Unnecessary Words	73, 77
40 Double Negatives	75, 96
41 Expressions to Be Avoided	74
42 Homophones	74, 84, 88, 96, 98
Sentences	
43 Fragments & Run-ons/ Kinds of Sentences	1, 2, 9, 11, 16, 22, 31, 42, 64, 89, 97, 98
44 Sentence Elements: Subject & Predicate	3, 6, 11, 14, 15, 19, 22, 24, 25, 33, 90, 94
45 Direct, Indirect Object/ Predicate Noun, Adjective	3, 4, 5, 6, 11, 14, 15, 19, 24, 25, 33, 35, 44, 90, 94, 98
46 Sentence Structure	12, 13, 15, 22, 67, 68, 69, 70, 71, 72, 77, 89, 92, 94, 98
47 Paragraphs	10, 21, 32, 43, 54, 82
48 Business Letters	79, 80, 87, 88, 97
Using a Dictionary	
49 Uses	78, 80, 86
50 Alphabetical Order	62, 86
51 Syllables	86
52 Pronunciation	86
53 Spelling	80
54 Speaking & Listening	Oral language development is supported throughout the lessons.

Teacher's Guide Organization

The *Practical Guide to Better English* **Teacher's Guide** for each level includes the following resources for teaching and managing the program:

OVERVIEW

- **Overviews** of the program, the student book, and the teacher's guide.

SCOPE AND SEQUENCE

- **Scope and Sequence Chart** of the grammar, usage, and mechanics skills taught in each level.

CORRELATION

- **Correlation** between the Handbook topics and individual lessons for that level.

PROCEDURES

- A **description of the five-step process of teaching a unit:** administering the diagnostic test; presenting each individual skill lesson; teaching the writing lesson; using the review lesson; and administering the achievement test.

- A **description of the basic sequence for presenting a lesson:** introducing the skill; directing students to the instructional text; previewing the content; assigning the lesson items; checking answers; assigning additional activities; and reviewing the lesson.

- **Suggestions for introducing the program** to students.

- **Descriptions of instructional procedures and options for meeting students' individual needs:** tips for classroom management; for promoting oral language development; for teaching composition; for adapting lessons to meet students' individual needs; and for helping students who are acquiring English.

- **Procedures and materials for evaluation of student progress:** suggested informal and formal assessment methods; reproducible blackline masters of diagnostic and achievement tests for each unit; a reproducible record-keeping form for tracking individual progress; and a rubric and checklists for use in evaluating the writing lessons.

ANSWER KEYS

- **Answer keys** for diagnostic and achievement tests and for student book lessons.

INDEX

- **Index of topical content** of individual lessons in the student book for that level.

How to Teach a Unit

Level IV of *Practical Guide to Better English* includes eight instructional units and a final review unit. The units are developmental and are intended to be taught in the order in which they are presented. Nevertheless, it is entirely appropriate to present lessons—or units—in any order that fits with your instructional goals. Each lesson in the program can stand alone because each is fully supported by instructions in the Handbook.

Each unit will take about three weeks to teach. The pace can easily be slowed or accelerated, however, to fit with students' progress.

Practical Guide to Better English
UNIT PLANNER
Option 1: Daily Practice

	MONDAY	TUESDAY	WEDNESDAY	THURSDAY	FRIDAY
Week 1	Diagnostic Test	Lesson 1	Lesson 2	Lesson 3	Lesson 4
Week 2	Lesson 5	Lesson 6	Lesson 7	Lesson 8	Lesson 9
Week 3	Composition Planning and Writing	Composition Revision	Composition Presentation	Review Lesson	Achievement Test

Practical Guide to Better English
UNIT PLANNER
Option 2: Three-Day-a-Week Practice

	MONDAY	TUESDAY	WEDNESDAY	THURSDAY	FRIDAY
Week 1	Diagnostic Test/ Lesson 1		Lesson 2		Lesson 3
Week 2	Lesson 4		Lesson 5		Lesson 6
Week 3	Lesson 7		Lesson 8		Lesson 9
Week 4	Composition Planning and Writing		Composition Revision and Presentation/ Review Lesson		Achievement Test

The recommended procedure for teaching a unit involves these five steps:

1. Administer the diagnostic test.

The diagnostic test for each unit can be used to measure what students know at the *beginning* of a unit. The diagnostic test should be administered before students begin working on the unit skill lessons. Students' performance on a diagnostic test can be compared with their performance on the achievement test, given at the end of the unit. Reproducible masters for the diagnostic tests begin on page 24 of this teacher's guide. A reproducible record-keeping form for the diagnostic and achievement tests is included on page 60.

2. Present each individual skill lesson.

Each unit contains nine skill lessons. It is recommended that one lesson be taught each day. Suggested procedures for presenting a lesson appear in the next section of this teacher's guide. The time required to teach a particular lesson will vary according to the difficulty of the concept, the nature of the practice, the instructional procedures used, and the students' ability.

3. Teach the writing lesson.

Each instructional unit contains a two-page writing lesson following the regular skill lessons. These activities lead students step-by-step through the task of writing and revising original compositions. A writing lesson can be completed in two or three class periods, depending on the available time and the students' writing proficiency. Each writing lesson has been designed so that students can complete it independently; however, some students may need additional guidance. Suggested procedures for presenting the writing lessons appear on pages 18–19 of this teacher's guide. A rubric for evaluating compositions and checklists for scoring the writing lessons can be found on pages 61-65.

4. Assign the review lesson.

A review lesson at the end of each instructional unit briefly covers the skills and concepts taught in the lessons. The review lesson is designed to reinforce learning and also indicate areas in which students may need remediation. Class time remaining after administering and checking the review lesson should be used to provide students with help on the skills they have not fully grasped, which should include careful review of the Handbook sections that instruct those skills.

5. Administer the achievement test.

At the conclusion of each unit, a two-page achievement test should be administered to all students. Reproducible masters for the achievement tests begin on page 26 of this teacher's guide. Students' performance on this test can be compared with their performance on the diagnostic test to measure progress. The reproducible record-keeping form on page 60 of this guide may be used to keep track of student progress. For more information on assessment procedures and options, see "Assessment" on pages 22–23 of this teacher's guide.

How to Present a Lesson

Each unit in Level IV of *Practical Guide to Better English* includes nine skill lessons. All lessons have a common structure that allows for as much or as little teacher guidance as a teacher chooses to provide.

The teaching procedure outlined here calls for teacher guidance throughout the lesson. Although it requires more time and direct involvement, this procedure offers a number of benefits: more opportunities for oral language development, effective use of scaffolding, modeling of correct English usage, constructive feedback, and authentic ongoing assessment. This procedure is especially recommended for use in the first few weeks of the school term, and whenever challenging new grammar concepts are being introduced.

If teacher involvement is impractical, students can be directed to complete the skill lessons independently. *All lessons in this program are written to be self-directing.* In addition, the Handbook serves as a dependable source of information for students working on their own. The more students use the Handbook as a resource, the better prepared they will be for success on the job, where the ability to use information in a manual or a handbook is a key to advancement.

Additional suggestions for presenting skill lessons are included in the sections of this teacher's guide that focus on managing classrooms, developing oral language, adapting lessons to meet individual needs, and helping students who are acquiring English.

RECOMMENDED SEQUENCE

1. **Introduce the skill.** Read the lesson title aloud. Engage students by asking questions that will help them make connections to previous lessons and prior knowledge. For example, for the lesson entitled "Punctuation" you might ask, *"What punctuation marks have you already studied? Which of these are used at the end of a sentence? Which are used to separate words or phrases within a sentence? Which are used to set off the words a person spoke?"*

2. **Direct students to the instructional text.** Point out the Handbook Guide(s) listed in the gray box. If a rule statement is given in the box, ask a volunteer to read it aloud. Next, have students find the guide(s) in their Handbooks, read the instructional text, complete the practice items, and check their answers. (If the practice items have been completed previously, have students review just the rules and the examples.) Students who are unable to complete the Handbook practice items successfully may need special help before they begin working on the lesson.

3. **Preview the content.** Discuss with students the lesson topic. This can be determined by skimming the exercise sentences. The "Index of Topics Featured in Level IV" at the end of this teacher's guide may also be used to identify the topic. Invite students to share what they already know about the topic. For example, for the lesson that tells about the sport of lacrosse, you might ask: *"What do you already know about the sport of lacrosse? How is it played? What equipment is used? What skills does a person need in order to be a good lacrosse player?"* By helping students focus on the content topic and building their background knowledge, you increase the likelihood that they will read the lesson items with good comprehension and become engaged with the language and content of the lesson.

4. **Assign the items.** Read aloud the instructions. Invite a volunteer to copy the example items on the chalkboard. Read aloud the items, describe how you would decide on the correct response, and model how you would write your response on the board. Then ask students to complete the lesson items independently or with partners.

5. **Check answers.** Invite volunteers to give their responses to the items orally; have students check their own work. Use the lesson answer key at the end of this teacher's guide to verify that responses given by students are correct. Invite students to ask questions about items they found difficult or confusing.

6. **Assign the additional section or vocabulary activity.** If the lesson has a Part II activity or a vocabulary puzzler, read aloud the instructions for it and discuss any examples. Next, have students complete the activity independently or with a partner. Then have volunteers give their answers while students check their own work. For those Part II activities that ask students to write original sentences, you may want to evaluate responses yourself.

7. **Review the lesson.** Have students count their correct responses and record their score at the top of the page and also on the score chart on page 176 of their books. Then invite one student to restate the rules and concepts learned in the lesson and tell how he or she can put these to use in writing and speaking.

Introducing the Program to Students

Teachers report that high school and adult students generally work more productively in courses in which the goals, instructional focus, procedures, and benefits are outlined in advance. Accordingly, you may want to use the following sequence to introduce *Practical Guide to Better English* to students.

1. Preview. Invite students to preview the book and talk about what they notice. Point out the goal statement at the beginning of "A Note to Students," which appears before the Contents page.

2. Set goals. Ask students to suggest reasons why it is important to be able to speak and write effectively using correct English. Record their reasons on the chalkboard. Then suggest to students that they choose one or more of these reasons as their personal goals and write these on a sheet of paper.

3. Look at one lesson. Have students all turn to one instructional lesson, such as Lesson 7, on page 11 of their books. Point out the *lesson title*, which gives the skill focus. Then point out the shaded box with the *listing of Handbook Guides*. Explain that these Handbook Guides have the rules and information they will need to learn in order to complete the lessons. Point out that the box also contains a rule reminder. Next, point out the instructions for the lesson and the examples of how to complete the items. Finally, point out the numbered *lesson items* and the *vocabulary puzzler* entitled "Synonym Watch."

4. Look at the Handbook. Explain to students that the Handbook is a reference they can use to learn and check what is correct English. Remind students that each lesson has a listing of the Handbook Guides they will need to study for that lesson. Have them turn to the Handbook Guides listed for Lesson 7—Guides 23 and 24*a*—*g*. Have volunteers read aloud the guides and orally complete the practice items. Then point out the answers; explain to students that as they read the guide sections, they should complete the practice items and check their answers to make sure they understand the rules.

5. Model the procedure for completing a lesson independently. Have a volunteer read aloud the steps for completing the lessons on page 2 of the student book. After each step is read, describe how you would carry this out for Lesson 5.

6. Look at one writing lesson. Explain to students that in addition to learning the rules of written English, they will have several opportunities to put the rules into action by writing their own compositions. Inform them that there are eight writing lessons in the book, and that each one teaches a particular kind of writing.

Introduce the writing lessons by having students turn to Lesson 32 of Unit III, "Writing an Explanation," on pages 38–39. Point out the *lesson title*. Then point out the bulleted list of *tips*. Explain that each writing lesson has a list of guidelines for the type of writing focused on in the lesson. Direct students' attention to the *writing model* and explain that it is an example of the writing form. As they write their own biography, they can look at the model for help. Finally, point out the heading *Write an Explanation* on page 39. Explain that these sections guide them through the steps of writing this composition. Point out that they will write their compositions on another piece of paper.

7. Discuss assessment procedures. Explain to students that they will take a test at the beginning and end of each unit. The diagnostic test at the beginning of each unit will indicate what they already know about the skills and rules that will be taught in the unit. The achievement test at the end of each unit will show what they have learned. Then tell students that in addition to the test the following activities will be evaluated: the sentences and paragraphs they write; how well they are able to revise and correct their work; how effectively they speak and listen; and their scores on the instructional lessons and review lessons.

Explain that these assessments can help identify concepts and rules they don't fully understand and skills they have not yet mastered. Assure students that you will work with them to help them master the skills and concepts that initially cause them problems.

Tips for Classroom Management

The *Practical Guide to Better English* program requires minimal teacher direction. As a result, it helps solve classroom management problems rather than create them. *All lessons in the program are self-instructive*, so students can be directed to work independently, or in pairs or small groups, while you work with the rest of the class on another task. The self-instructive nature of the lessons, plus the support for independent learning provided by the Handbook, allow for great flexibility in pacing and grouping, as described in the following sections.

Flexibility. The program provides a year's course of study. Lessons are developmental, and spiral learning occurs within and across levels to reinforce concepts and skills. The program can be easily adapted to suit the needs of individual classrooms because *every skill lesson can stand alone*. The Handbook Guides referenced in each lesson provide students with the concepts and rules they need to complete the lesson successfully. Further, since the Handbook itself is organized in sensible sequence to explain grammar, usage, and mechanics concepts, students who find themselves unsure of how a particular rule fits in the greater fabric of correct English can read the Handbook Guide sections before and after the sections referenced to gain a better understanding.

As you use this level of *Practical Guide to Better English* in your classroom, feel free to expand, drop, or change the order of lessons. Your sense of what will be of greatest value to your students is the best guide to what lessons should be taught when.

Pacing. Because the skill lessons in *Practical Guide to Better English* are self-instructive and free-standing, the program offers more pacing options than comparable programs. Among these options are the following:

- The whole class can proceed at a single pace.

- Students can be grouped heterogeneously, and all groups can proceed at a similar pace.

- Students can be grouped homogeneously, and each group can proceed at a pace appropriate for its members.

- Students who need work on all skills and concepts can work through the program

together at a steady pace. Students who have greater proficiency can work on just those lessons that focus on problems that show up in their written work.

- All students can work at their own pace, checking in with you each time they are ready to begin or conclude a unit.

Grouping. Most students will benefit from working with other students at least part of the time. Group work offers opportunities for oral language development, cooperative problem-solving, peer tutoring and counseling, shared reading, and oral presentation of written work to an audience. Each mode offers particular advantages:

- Working in *small heterogeneous groups* allows students with less advanced literacy skills to benefit from the modeling and mentoring of more proficient students. In turn, the more proficient students develop communication skills and strengthen their own knowledge of grammar, usage, and mechanics principles as they work to convey these concepts to others in the group.

- Working in *small homogeneous groups* offers greater opportunities for providing scaffolding. (See "Adapting Lessons to Meet Students' Individual Needs" on pages 20–21 of this teacher's guide.) Many teachers report that students are most comfortable and work most productively in groups in which other students have the same level of proficiency. In part this may be because members of such groups can all contribute to the problem-solving process—none of them has all the answers.

- Working in *pairs* encourages thought and dialogue. Many of the skills activities in the lessons in *Practical Guide to Better English* lend themselves to partnered learning. Pairs of students working on the same lesson can share prior knowledge of the skill and the lesson topic, and read and discuss the Handbook Guides together. They can work independently on the exercise items, and then reconvene to check answers and help each other clear up any areas of confusion.

Promoting Oral Language Development

The process of acquiring English language skills begins with oral language development. Students need to hear correct language patterns, and practice producing these in their own speech, in order to internalize the patterns and employ them in their writing.

Oral communication is of particular benefit to students with limited fluency and knowledge of the English language because it allows them to experiment with language in a setting that is less formal and less threatening than written formats. At the same time, oral language activities—listening as well as speaking—expand students' vocabularies, which is essential for their educational progress and eventual success in the working world.

In order to develop oral language skills, students should have opportunities to do these things:

- Listen and speak for a **variety of purposes**: give directions, seek information, express opinions, respond to requests.

- Listen to and contribute ideas **in various settings**: one-to-one, small-group, and whole-class discussions.

- Listen and speak to share **knowledge about lesson topics.**

- Listen to and read aloud **models of basic grammatical structures** in order to gain oral fluency using proper syntax.

- Listen to and repeat **accurate pronunciation of words** in order to achieve effective oral communication.

- Listen to and discuss the **differences between formal and informal language** and the settings in which each is appropriate.

- Listen to and repeat examples of the **diversity of language** and recognize how it is used for different purposes and audiences in various types of communication.

The instructional skill lessons in *Practical Guide to Better English* offer many opportunities for listening and speaking:

- When a skill lesson is first presented, students can **share knowledge and opinions about the lesson topics.**

- During the lesson introduction, students can **read aloud rule statements, discuss examples, suggest other examples orally, or complete the Handbook practice activities orally.**

- As the class prepares to complete the skill lesson, students can **read aloud the instructions or the lesson sentences.**

- After students complete the lesson, they can **give correct answers orally and explain how they decided that they were correct.**

- Prior to completing open-ended exercise items (writing sentences with a certain grammatical element, combining sentences, and so on), students can **read aloud the items and discuss possible responses to each.**

- If the lesson offers a vocabulary extension activity, students can **solve the vocabulary puzzler orally.**

- As an extension activity, students inspired by the topic of a particular lesson can **prepare and present brief oral reports.**

The writing lessons also offer opportunities for productive oral expression:

- When a writing form is introduced, students can **share what they know** about that form and discuss any writing or reading experiences they may have had with that type of writing.

- Students can **read the writing model aloud** and share their reactions. For instance, after reading a persuasive paragraph, they might give their own opinions about the issue. After reading a science report, they might share other facts they know about the topic.

- Students can **orally answer the questions** that ask them to identify specific elements in the model.

- As they plan their own writing, students can work cooperatively to **brainstorm topic ideas** or **discuss the sequence of ideas** that might work best for expository or narrative compositions.

- Revising written work offers students the opportunity to **give and receive constructive feedback**: students can trade drafts and **offer suggestions** for revision.

- Students can **read aloud their completed writing**; listeners can **give their reactions.**

- Process writing lessons also offer students multiple opportunities for oral expression as they **brainstorm, revise,** and **publish** their work.

Teaching Composition

The writing component of *Practical Guide to Better English* offers students the opportunity to apply grammar, usage, and mechanics skills in the context of original compositions. Authentic writing activities ask students to draw upon their own experiences, opinions, interests, and ideas, as well as factual information from the content areas. They can use these experiences as they learn to construct paragraphs, essays, reports, narratives, and other standard forms of writing required for success in school, on state assessment tests, in daily life, and in the workplace.

The Domains of Writing. The domains of writing are generally (although not universally) identified as **expository, persuasive, narrative,** and **descriptive.** The writing lessons in *Practical Guide to Better English* reflect the writing requirements and domains currently in use in many states across the country. The lessons are designed to help students understand that each form of writing has its own purpose, audience, and structure. The forms listed in the chart below are taught in the *Practical Guide to Better English* writing lessons.

Program Goals. The writing exercises and lessons of *Practical Guide to Better English* are designed to help students develop writing fluency at the sentence, paragraph, and whole composition levels. The program is developmental in nature, beginning with simple tasks and progressing to more challenging ones—both within and across grade levels. The lessons are designed to help students develop these skills:

- Write in a variety of circumstances: in response to questions that require single-sentence answers; to writing prompts that require a response of one or more paragraphs; and to longer, more formal assignments.

- Use the steps of the writing process.

- Revise writing based on feedback and reflection.

- Use the conventions of grammar and spelling, and develop good proofreading habits.

- Write for real-life situations: college or job applications, letters, resumes, and so on.

Process Writing vs. Demand Writing. Of the eight writing lessons presented in each level of *Practical Guide to Better English*, two take students through the steps of the writing process. The other six lessons guide students in developing shorter compositions, what some researchers call *demand writing*. Demand writing requires students to develop a clear, cohesive response to a specific writing prompt, in a controlled setting, often in a limited amount of time. Preparation for statewide writing proficiency tests is one good reason to teach demand writing; another is its wealth of real-life applications. As adults, students will engage in demand writing in most cases when writing is required—when composing letters, filling out job applications, giving directions and explanations, and in many other everyday tasks.

The writing lessons in Units IV and VIII teach students a useful method for developing longer, more complex compositions, such as research reports, essays, and narratives.

EXPOSITORY	PERSUASIVE	NARRATIVE	DESCRIPTIVE
compare/contrast (III)	**persuasive paragraph** (I, II)	**personal narrative** (I, II, III)	descriptive sentences (I)
research report (I, III)	**persuasive essay** (IV)	**story—narrative elements** (I, II, IV)	descriptive paragraph (I, II)
summary (I, III)	product endorsement (III)		descriptive composition (III)
how-to paragraph (I, II)	résumé (IV)		descriptive essay (IV)
problem/solution (II, IV)	**letter of application for employment** (IV)		
paragraph of information (II)			
explanation (II, IV)			
biography (III)			
news articles (III)			

(Assignments that appear in boldface type are presented as process writing activities at least once in the program. Numbers in parentheses indicate at which level[s] the writing form is taught.)

TEACHING THE WRITING LESSONS

Each writing lesson is designed so that students can complete it independently. However, some students may need additional support. Here are some suggestions for adapting the writing lessons for students with differing needs:

Students Acquiring English. In the sequence of language acquisition, writing fluency is usually the last skill second-language learners acquire. When teaching composition to students acquiring English, help them develop ideas and try out sentence structures by offering opportunities for oral language expression before, during, and after writing. (See the section entitled "Promoting Oral Language Development" in this teacher's guide for oral language opportunities in the writing lessons.)

Here are some additional procedures that can help second-language learners:

- **Determine students' writing fluency in their native language.** Ask students to describe writing they have done. Have them describe the processes they use when they write. (Example: *If you wanted to compare a lion and a tiger, how would you do it in writing?*) If students possess writing fluency in their native language, they are likely to need less instruction on the structure of the various writing forms taught in this program.

- **Provide support with syntax.** Students acquiring English are likely to struggle with usage issues such as subject-verb agreement, pronoun use, article use, verb forms, and sentence structure. Have students identify and tag the Handbook Guides that focus on these, and remind them to refer to those sections often. In addition, you may need to assign specific usage lessons a second time.

- **Pair each second-language learner with a partner who is fluent in English.** Have the partner read aloud the writing model, and have the student acquiring English retell it orally. Partners can then discuss the writing assignment together and talk about what they plan to write. The second-language learner can dictate his or her paragraph(s). Partners should work together to proofread and correct their work.

Students with Little or No Writing Experience. Students with limited writing experience often have little idea of how to begin a writing assignment; they also typically do not know what is expected in terms of the product. Group these students *homogeneously* and go through the first several writing assignments with them, modeling how you would complete each step. Then walk students through the lesson again, this time having students complete the various parts of the writing activity as a group. It is particularly important for these students to spend time thinking about how the writing model is structured because they bring little knowledge with them about the organization and purpose of different writing forms. As students gain confidence as writers and familiarity with the various domains, gradually encourage them to tackle the writing lessons in pairs or independently.

Students with Poor Reading Fluency. Some students who are poor readers can be quite successful at writing, with guidance and encouragement. It may benefit these students to complete the writing activities with a *peer partner* who has good reading skills, but may be a less fluent writer or inventive thinker. That student can read the tips, writing model, and instructions aloud, and the partners can help each other plan and write their paragraphs.

Reluctant Writers. Students who display a reluctance to write may be encouraged to begin by writing only a small amount—perhaps just one sentence. You may need to work with these students *individually.* Encourage all efforts, no matter how minimal the outcome may seem: one sentence is a beginning! Gradually, encourage students to add sentences until they are composing complete paragraphs. Alternately, you might put off teaching the writing lessons until later in the year, when students' writing fluency at the sentence level has increased and their confidence as writers has improved.

Special Help for Nonproductive Writers. Students who possess little writing fluency frequently feel intimidated by even simple writing tasks, and often bring with them years of frustration and discouragement. Here are some additional suggestions for helping these students:

- Praise students' attempts, especially at the beginning. Point out strengths in their written work *before* helping them find areas that need improvement. Assure students that their writing will improve, and that writing is a skill that takes time and practice to learn.

- Guide students to see that *writing is a process that begins with thinking*, and help them learn organizational strategies that allow them to collect their thoughts before they write.

- Often, a composition that is weak in many ways nonetheless contains one element that is particularly praiseworthy: a descriptive phrase that is especially colorful; a unique word choice; a powerful or moving sentence about an event. Look for these "unexpected gems" and share them with the class. Reading these passages aloud will demonstrate some elements of good writing and boost the confidence of less fluent writers. Try to read from every student's work at least once. Telling students that any student work that is read aloud will be read anonymously will help them feel comfortable with this practice.

- Start slowly, and build over time. Adapt the sequence and complexity of writing activities to match your students' abilities. Move from sentence to paragraph to composition slowly, recognizing that different students will progress at different paces. When students do show increased fluency and confidence, though, be sure to offer them writing assignments that challenge them appropriately, while providing the support they will need to succeed on these. (See "Adapting Lessons to Meet Students' Individual Needs" in this teacher's guide for a discussion of scaffolding.)

EVALUATION AND ASSESSMENT

Establishing a Baseline. At the beginning of the school year you may wish to establish the baseline proficiency of the students in your class. This will help you assess individual students' strengths and weaknesses, and may help you employ grouping strategies that will help your students grow as writers. To establish a baseline, give all students the same writing prompt to respond to. The prompt should not require any specialized knowledge or vocabulary. (Example: *What is your earliest memory? Write about it.*) Responses will give you an indication of each student's writing fluency. Compare this initial assignment with subsequent writing efforts to help you assess progress.

Using a Rubric and Checklists to Evaluate Writing. A rubric that can be used to help you evaluate the overall quality of students' compositions has been provided on page 61 of this teacher's guide. Evaluation checklists, which have been provided for each writing lesson in the student book, begin on page 62 of this teacher's guide. It is recommended that you duplicate a set of these checklists for each student at the beginning of the year; they will serve as both evaluation and record-keeping forms.

Student Self-Evaluation. Periodically, have students compare their early work with their later writing so that they, too, can be aware of their growth as writers. You may choose occasionally to have more fluent writers use the checklists to evaluate their own work. Alternately, have more advanced students construct their own criteria by asking them questions such as: *What makes an outstanding personal narrative?* Encourage students to use their criteria as guides when evaluating their own work and the work of their peers.

REMEDIATION AND PRACTICE

Grammar and Mechanics. Most developing writers need ongoing practice with basic grammar and mechanics skills, such as avoiding run-ons and sentence fragments, using high-utility homophones such as *it's* and *its* properly, and using commas correctly. As you identify specific skills that need improvement, assign one or more of the following remediation activities:

- Have students review the appropriate section(s) of the Handbook and study the practice exercises. Give them five additional practice items to complete for each skill.

- Have students complete a lesson that focuses on the targeted skill a second time. Repeat this until students can answer each item correctly.

- Help students create a list of their own "trouble spots," including references to the Handbook Guides, and use the list whenever they revise their writing. As they achieve mastery with specific skills, they can remove those "trouble spots" from the list.

Content. Developing writers often struggle with organizing and sequencing the flow of their ideas. Help them to see writing as a thinking process. Visual mapping activities such as word webs, outlines, and Venn diagrams can help students organize their thoughts and understand the vital connection between thinking and writing. If possible, evaluate completed writing with students individually. Help them identify ideas that are repeated, contradictory, out of sequence, or off the topic. Then have students rewrite the piece, based on their own observations.

Practice. Following are some suggestions for helping students practice their writing and revising skills outside the lessons:

- Provide additional writing prompts to reinforce demand writing skills. Encourage students to make a habit of using the *Plan* and *Write* steps to help them organize their thoughts quickly before they begin writing.

- Have students rewrite exercise sentences from an instructional lesson as paragraphs, adding transition words, an introduction, and a conclusion. Encourage them to consider resequencing the sentences to improve the flow of ideas.

- To provide proofreading practice, pair students and have each one rewrite a paragraph from a book, omitting all punctuation and capitalization and inserting some spelling errors. Partners can trade passages, correct them, and then check their work against the original passage.

Adapting Lessons to Meet Students' Individual Needs

Students learn best when lessons encourage them to stretch for new knowledge *that is within their reach if they stretch.* This process of having to work to grasp a concept ensures engagement, develops thinking processes, and prepares the student for the next stretch he or she will need to make.

Education researchers, such as Dr. Robert Rueda of the University of Southern California, have explained the process of supporting students' learning as being similar to constructing **scaffolding.** The best kind of help puts each student within reach—but not always easy reach—of important concepts and information.

What makes this process challenging for a teacher are the many differences among students in any class. Students bring with them widely differing literacy skills and background knowledge; they learn in different ways, and they learn at different paces. Adjusting each lesson to provide just the right amount of challenge to each student is a goal unlikely to be met in a real-world classroom.

Nevertheless, you can make instruction significantly more effective by keeping in mind the effectiveness of scaffolding and becoming aware of students' preferred modes of learning and varying levels of proficiency.

ADDRESSING THE THREE MODALITIES

Over the years many teachers have found it helpful to tailor some activities to students who learn best *visually,* some to students who learn best *aurally,* and some to students who learn best *kinesthetically.* Lessons in *Practical Guide to Better English* can be adapted in a number of ways to address each of these modalities. Here are a few suggestions:

Visual. As a part of each lesson on sentence structure, show students how to diagram a simple sentence with that structure. Diagramming was formerly thought of by some as tedious and esoteric; and it can be, with complex sentences. But a sentence diagram is actually a graphic organizer—a highly visual way of illustrating how basic sentence elements relate to one another. Showing students how to diagram simple sentences is likely to be of great help to those who are visual learners.

Aural. In lessons on parts of speech and on related word forms, read aloud lesson sentences using nonsense substitutions to highlight functions and inflected endings.

The *bink binked* a *bink.*

The *bink binked binkly.*

The *binky bink* was *binked* by a *bink.*

Students can be asked to replace the nonsense forms with real words, and explain how they decided what kind of word to use.

Kinesthetic. To help students understand how different parts of speech and kinds of phrases function in sentences, have students cut sentences from the lesson apart into words and phrases, and then see how many sentences *different from the originals* they can put together using clear tape.

ADAPTING LESSONS FOR STUDENTS WITH LESS PROFICIENCY

Users of this program are likely to have already developed a number of effective ways to help less advanced students gain benefit from lessons they are unable to complete independently. Following are some suggestions that may or may not be new to you.

- Read Handbook sections, lesson directions, and any examples aloud. Have a volunteer write the first lesson item on the board and model completing it. Then have students work in pairs to complete the lesson items.

- Have students work in a small group led by a peer tutor. Group members can take turns completing items, showing their responses to the group, and explaining their answer choices.

- Using the chalkboard, model completing the first five items of a lesson. Have students watch with their books closed. Then have them open their books and work on those same five items, plus the next five. Have them then stop, check, and discuss their work. Finally, have them complete the remaining items.

- For the first item, write a correct response and an incorrect response on the chalkboard. Have students raise their hands when you point to the response they believe is correct. Ask a student who identified the correct response to tell why it is correct. Continue this process until students seem confident they can complete the remaining items independently.

Helping Students Who Are Acquiring English

Older students who are acquiring English face a special challenge. The content load of the texts for which they are responsible in classes or on the job is typically heavy, but their oral and written English skills may be at a relatively low level. Yet they have a compelling need to understand and make use of the information in such texts because long-term success in the workplace depends on their being able to do so.

For these students to have the best possible chance of succeeding in a course of study, both the materials and the instruction must be considerate of their needs and abilities. Simplicity and clarity are extremely important. As Robert Rueda, professor of educational psychology at the University of Southern California has written, "Trying to learn difficult academic content at the same time one is trying to understand an unfamiliar language tends to overload the capacity to learn."

The lessons and Handbook Guides in the *Practical Guide to Better English* program have been written and structured to meet the needs of second language learners and their teachers. Every effort has been made to simplify language and structure and eliminate obstacles to understanding. Nevertheless, because the program deals with a complex subject—the structure and rules of the English language—students acquiring English are likely to experience some language-related difficulties in the course of completing lessons. Your ability to recognize that a student is having difficulty and offer appropriate help is one of the most important elements in the instructional process. The teaching procedures listed below have been shown to be of significant value to second language learners, both in helping them complete coursework successfully and in advancing their acquisition of English.

ORAL LANGUAGE DEVELOPMENT

- Read aloud examples and answers.

- Ask students to answer items orally.

- Model effective oral reading and pronunciation by reading passages aloud.

- Use repetition—have students repeat what they hear.

- For those students with lesser levels of English proficiency, have them respond orally to questions whose answers they have already learned.

VOCABULARY DEVELOPMENT

- Identify and review key vocabulary and concepts for exercises; write these words on the chalkboard; use pictures or props to illustrate word meanings when possible.

- Discuss the meanings of unfamiliar expressions and idioms.

- Discuss troublesome words: multiple meaning words, homophones, and homographs. Guide students to use context to determine meaning.

- Direct students to develop webs of related words for use in writing activities.

- Encourage students to keep lists of words they want to make part of their active vocabulary; encourage them to use these in class discussions and writing activities.

CONCEPT DEVELOPMENT AND SKILL INSTRUCTION (SCAFFOLDING)

- Activate students' prior knowledge of familiar subjects through class discussion.

- Discuss with students topics likely to be unfamiliar to them before directing them to read or write about those topics.

- Read aloud and model activities with volunteers.

- Redefine terms orally.

- Speak clearly and pause often.

- Say the same thing in different ways.

- Ask yes/no questions to engage students.

- Use visual learning cues—drawings, photographs, illustrations—when possible.

- Dramatize meaning through facial expressions, pantomime, and gestures.

- Check comprehension frequently by asking questions.

- Remind students of particular things to do or avoid doing.

- Have students dictate their ideas for writing activities before they begin the task of writing.

- Encourage students to make comparisons between their primary language and English.

COOPERATIVE LEARNING

- Have students work with English-proficient partners on proofreading activities.

- Offer opportunities for students who share the same primary language to work on skill lessons and activities together.

AWARENESS OF CULTURAL DIFFERENCES

- Be prepared for different personal responses to exercise items.

- Keep in mind that students' difficulties in responding to a lesson topic may be the result of cultural differences rather than lack of comprehension of vocabulary.

Assessment

A cornerstone of the *Practical Guide to Better English* program is ongoing assessment that provides a clear picture of each student's level of proficiency with specific English language skills and writing tasks. The program's formal assessment instruments enable you to adjust instruction in each unit to fit students' needs as well as monitor their progress. Informal assessment, which can take many forms, including those outlined on the next page, provides additional information about students' strengths and weaknesses. Assessment of the writing activities enables both teachers and students to recognize growth in language proficiency as well as identify areas in which more work is needed.

FORMAL ASSESSMENT IN *PRACTICAL GUIDE TO BETTER ENGLISH*

Diagnostic Tests. Each unit's diagnostic test provides a quick snapshot of students' familiarity with the skills covered in that unit. Reproducible masters of diagnostic tests for Units I–VIII appear on pages 24–53 in this teacher's guide. To administer the diagnostic text for a unit, give each student a copy of the test; have students complete all sections independently; then collect the tests and check students' answers. Answers to these tests appear on pages 56–57 of this teacher's guide. Afterward, look at each student's errors. On the basis of the patterns you note, you may want to adjust instruction in one of these ways:

- If a small group of students show by their responses that they are not at all familiar with a skill, you may want to provide a pre-lesson tutorial on that skill for those students.

- If the majority of the class indicate through their responses that they are not at all familiar with a skill that will be taught in the unit, you may want to utilize one of the whole-class guided learning procedures outlined in "Adapting Lessons to Meet Students' Individual Needs" when presenting that lesson.

- If some students show by their responses that they are already familiar with a skill to be taught, you may want to have them either skip that lesson, complete it as homework, or serve as peer tutors for that lesson to students who need work on that skill.

Be sure to retain students' tests so you can compare their performance on each section with their performance on the same section of the achievement test, which is to be administered at the conclusion of the unit. Use the record-keeping form on page 60 of this teacher's guide to record test scores.

Achievement Tests. Each unit's achievement test checks students' progress with the unit skills and provides information that can be used to develop a plan for targeted remediation and additional practice. Reproducible masters of achievement tests for Units I–VIII appear on pages 26–55 in this teacher's guide. Administer the achievement test for a unit in the same manner as the diagnostic test. Answers for these tests appear on pages 58–59. Afterward, compare each student's performance on each section with his or her performance on the same section of the diagnostic test. Note areas of progress and areas in which remedial work is needed. For students needing remediation in a particular skill, it is recommended that you repeat the lesson that focuses on the problem area, and have them work through the exercises a second time using one of the procedures outlined in the section headed "Adapting Lessons for Students with Less Proficiency" in this teacher's guide.

You may want to record each student's performance on the individual student record-keeping form on page 60 of this teacher's guide.

Writing Assessment. Suggestions for assessing students' writing progress appear in the section entitled "Teaching Composition" on pages 17–20 of this teacher's guide. A rubric and checklists for evaluating writing lessons appear on pages 61–65.

INFORMAL ASSESSMENT IN *PRACTICAL GUIDE TO BETTER ENGLISH*

Observation/Holistic Assessment. Observing and making note of individual students' performance on various tasks during the course of each unit is an important part of the assessment process.

Among the many productive focuses for informal observation are the following:

- Students' performance on the exercises, including how much help they need to be able to complete the exercises.

- Students' knowledge of grammar, usage, and mechanics concepts as evidenced in their responses to questions asked of them.

- Students' willingness to try using new vocabulary and specialized terms in oral discussions.

- Students' use of correct and incorrect word forms in class discussions.

- Students' use of correct and incorrect word forms in written work for literature study, and in papers written for other classes.

- Students' attitude toward completing the exercises and writing tasks.

- Students' choice of books and magazines for independent reading.

Space for recording observations and anecdotal records of progress is provided on the individual student record-keeping form.

Student Self-Monitoring. Students can monitor themselves as they work through the unit by making note of what they do and do not understand, either in a personal journal or directly on the lesson pages. Encourage them also to use the practice items in the Handbook Guides as a quick method of assessing whether they understand a new rule or concept. The score chart that appears on page 176 of the student book provides a further means for students to keep track of personal progress.

Name_____   Date _____

UNIT I
Diagnostic Test, *page 1*

PART I   Punctuate each group of words that is a sentence. Write *F* after each group of words that is a sentence fragment.

  1.   Travel by hot air balloon is exciting ___

  2.   A large striped balloon with a basket underneath ___

  3.   A basket is fastened to the balloon by ropes ___

  4.   Hundreds of feet above the ground ___

PART II   Punctuate each sentence. On the line, write the word *declarative, interrogative, exclamatory,* or *imperative* to show what kind of sentence it is.

  5.   Did you bring your binoculars__   _____

  6.   How small those sheep look__   _____

  7.   Give me the topographical map__   _____

  8.   We're floating over Forestville now__   _____

PART III   On the lines below each sentence, write the subject, the verb or verb phrase, and the direct object, in that order.

  9.   The wind controls the direction of the flight.

       _____   _____   _____

  10.   The pilot controls vertical movement.

       _____   _____   _____

  11.   Will has taken thirty pictures already.

       _____   _____   _____

PART IV   Underline each predicate noun. Circle each predicate adjective.

  12.   She is an industrious woman.

  13.   He is very artistic.

  14.   That was a terrible movie.

PRACTICAL GUIDE TO BETTER ENGLISH

PART V   Circle the direct object in each sentence. If the sentence has an indirect object, write it on the line.

15.   Alison gave me the tickets.   _____

16.   Will told his sister a scary story.   _____

17.   A farmer sold Paul some ripe tomatoes.   _____

PART VI   Draw one line under the simple subject in each sentence. Draw two lines under the simple predicate. Circle each direct object. Draw a box around each predicate noun and each predicate adjective.

18.   That balloon is particularly colorful.

19.   Mr. Pritchard has owned the company for six years.

20.   The company's best pilot is a woman from Iowa.

PART VII   Underline the word that correctly completes each sentence.

21.   The thought of a hot air balloon ride (doesn't, don't) scare me.

22.   (Is, Are) there any parachutes for rent?

23.   (Isn't, Aren't) Randy afraid of heights?

PART VIII   Underline each word that should begin with a capital letter.

24.   i've scheduled our balloon trip for sunday, may 16.

25.   our guide, mr. pritchard, is from aberdeen, scotland.

26.   his company is called limitless sky adventures.

27.   they have offices in albuquerque, topeka, and stillwater.

PART IX   Place punctuation marks where they belong in these sentences.

28.   Napa California is famous for ballooning explained Rick

29.   Rick have you ever flown a balloon asked Suzanne

30.   Rick replied Yes I've ballooned in Utah Nevada and Kansas

PRACTICAL GUIDE TO BETTER ENGLISH

UNIT 1
Achievement Test, page 1

PART I   Punctuate each group of words that is a sentence. Write *F* after each group of words that is a sentence fragment.

1. The wildlife in Australia is unusual ___

2. The red kangaroo, a large marsupial ___

3. Hopping swiftly on strong hind legs ___

4. All marsupials have pouches ___

PART II   Punctuate each sentence. On the line, write the word *declarative, interrogative, exclamatory,* or *imperative* to show what kind of sentence it is.

5. Tell me about platypuses__   _____

6. Did you know that they lay eggs__   _____

7. They swim underwater like seals__   _____

8. How strange this duckbilled mammal looks__   _____

PART III   On the lines below each sentence, write the subject, the verb or verb phrase, and the direct object, in that order.

9. Echidnas lay eggs, too.

   _____ _____ _____

10. These Australian mammals eat ants.

   _____ _____ _____

11. Their spines discourage most attackers.

   _____ _____ _____

PART IV   Underline each predicate noun. Circle each predicate adjective.

12. You are a clever person.

13. That is a valuable ring.

14. Your apartment is quite large.

PRACTICAL GUIDE TO BETTER ENGLISH

PART V Circle the direct object in each sentence. If the sentence has an indirect object, write it on the line.

15. Raquel sent me a postcard from Australia. _____

16. The koala fed her baby some leaves. _____

17. I bought my grandmother some roses. _____

PART VI Draw one line under the simple subject in each sentence. Draw two lines under the simple predicate. Circle each direct object. Draw a box around each predicate noun and each predicate adjective.

18. Marsupials are remarkable creatures.

19. I have been studying Australian wildlife for a year.

20. The platypus is unique among mammals.

PART VII Underline the word that correctly completes each sentence.

21. (Isn't, Aren't) the wallaby a marsupial?

22. (Is, Are) there any kingfishers in this region?

23. Virginia (think, thinks) Australia is fascinating.

PART VIII Underline each word that should begin with a capital letter.

24. on sunday, march 29, we watched a show at the international academy of science.

25. the narrator was dr. angela warren from sydney, australia.

26. some australian species are also native to new guinea.

27. dr. warren has attended conferences in north america, australia, and south america.

PART IX Place punctuation marks where they belong in these sentences.

28. Sydney Australia is situated on a large deep beautiful harbor said Jack

29. Jack don't the people of Sydney have an unusual nickname asked Wanda

30. Jack replied Yes the residents of Sydney are called *Sydneysiders*

PRACTICAL GUIDE TO BETTER ENGLISH

UNIT II
Diagnostic Test, page 1

PART I On the line after each sentence, tell whether the sentence is simple or compound. In every compound sentence, underline each complete thought and put parentheses around the conjunction.

1. Mt. St. Helens is in Washington State. _____

2. It was once a tall, pointed mountain, but volcanic activity changed its shape. _____

3. In 1980 a violent eruption took place. _____

4. The mountain rumbled for months, and finally the top blew off. _____

PART II Use the conjunction *and, but,* or *or* to combine each pair of short sentences into one compound sentence.

5. Scientists expected an eruption. Its suddenness surprised them.

   _____

6. A rumbling sound filled the air. Ash poured into the sky.

   _____

7. We could view photographs of the event. We could watch a videotape.

   _____

PART III Combine each pair of short sentences into one longer sentence. You can create compound subjects, compound predicates, or compound sentences.

8. Trees were incinerated. Animal habitats were destroyed.

   _____

9. The mountain spewed ash. The mountain belched smoke.

   _____

10. Scientists witnessed the eruption. Scientists studied its effects.

   _____

PART IV Shorten each sentence using a compound element.

11. Is that a bird, or is that a plane?

   _____

PRACTICAL GUIDE TO BETTER ENGLISH

12.   Did André take your coat, and did he offer you some lemonade?

_____

13.   The lemonade is cold, and it is delicious.

_____

PART V   Punctuate each sentence.

14.   Did lava cover the mountainsides or were some patches left unharmed

15.   Trees homes and roads were instantly destroyed

16.   Local residents had some warning luckily and took precautions

17.   How awful the destruction was

PART VI   Write a sentence using the word in parentheses in the form indicated.

18.   (man—*plural*)   _____

19.   (pony—*plural*)   _____

20.   (women—*possessive*)   _____

21.   (cars—*possessive*)   _____

PART VII   Write a phrase with a possessive noun to tell about each item described below.

22.   the shoes that belong to the girls   _____

23.   the songs played by the band   _____

24.   the sausages made by the butcher   _____

PART VIII   Underline each noun. On the line below the noun, write *subject*, *predicate noun*, *indirect object*, or *direct object* to show how the noun is used.

25.   The landscape was a desolate sight.

_____

26.   Ash covered the fields.

_____

27.   Dawn gave the land an eerie glow.

_____

PART IX   Draw a line under each word that should begin with a capital letter in the following paragraph. Add appropriate punctuation.

28–30.
        after a few years, signs of life began to return to mt st helens seedlings poked up through the ash deer squirrels and foxes began to return the people of washington must have been quite relieved that the lifeless state was not permanent homes have not been built near the blast zone however scientists believe that mt saint helens will erupt again sometime in the future

PRACTICAL GUIDE TO BETTER ENGLISH

UNIT II
Achievement Test, *page 1*

PART I   On the line after each sentence, tell whether the sentence is simple or compound. In every compound sentence, underline each complete thought and put parentheses around the conjunction.

1.   Ants live in colonies.   _____

2.   The queen lays eggs, and workers keep the colony running.   _____

3.   An ant colony has different chambers for different purposes.   _____

4.   Most ants are a dull color, but some are colorful.   _____

PART II   Use the conjunction *and*, *but*, or *or* to combine each pair of short sentences into one compound sentence.

5.   Male ants are larger than workers. They are smaller than queens.

_____

6.   That could be a harvester ant. It could be a weaver ant.

_____

7.   Ants are social. They are loyal to their colony.

_____

PART III   Combine each pair of short sentences into one longer sentence. You can create compound subjects, compound predicates, or compound sentences.

8.   Army ants march in swarms. Army ants eat any insects in their path.

_____

9.   Male ants have wings. Queens have wings.

_____

10.   Ants' nests have many tunnels. They also have many chambers.

_____

PART IV   Shorten each sentence using a compound element.

11.   Is an anthill more like a beehive, or is an anthill more like a spider nest?

_____

PRACTICAL GUIDE TO BETTER ENGLISH

12.   Workers build the nest, and they care for the young.

_____

13.   Soldier ants are large, and they are fierce.

_____

PART V   Punctuate each sentence.

14.   Are there ants in the cupboard again or are you shrieking about something else

15.   This time they're in the honey the sugar and the cereal

16.   Ants love those foods of course and anything else sweet

17.   What a mess this is

PART VI   Write a sentence using the word in parentheses in the form indicated.

18.   (mouse—*plural*)   _____

19.   (butterfly—*plural*)   _____

20.   (children—*possessive*)   _____

21.   (ants—*possessive*)   _____

PART VII   Write a phrase with a possessive noun to tell about each item described below.

22.   the nest that belongs to the ants   _____

23.   the sandwiches brought by the family   _____

24.   the trail made by the insects   _____

PART VIII   Underline each noun. On the line below the noun, write *subject, predicate noun, indirect object,* or *direct object* to show how the noun is used.

25.   A soldier gave her enemy a shove.

_____

26.   The ant was defending her colony.

_____

27.   Some ants are ferocious fighters.

_____

PART IX   Draw a line under each word that should begin with a capital letter in the following paragraph. Add appropriate punctuation.

28–30.
     leaf-cutter ants live in parts of south america they cut pieces of leaves carry them to their nest and chew them into pulp the ants use this pulp to fertilize fungus gardens the fungi produce tiny knobs, which the ants eat brazilian leaf-cutter ants are considered pests because they strip leaves from orange trees and other crops

PRACTICAL GUIDE TO BETTER ENGLISH

UNIT III
Diagnostic Test, *page 1*

PART I   Read each pair of sentences. Underline each noun in the first sentence. In the second sentence, underline each pronoun that has replaced a noun.

1. Gayle bought a violin.
   She bought it.

2. The guitars are made of rosewood.
   They are made of rosewood.

3. Many musicians practice scales regularly.
   They practice them regularly.

4. Raul is learning to play the piano.
   He is learning to play it.

PART II   Think about how each underlined pronoun is used in these sentences. Then draw a line under the word or phrase in parentheses that tells how the pronoun is used.

5. I performed at a jazz club last week. (direct object, subject)

6. My brother saw me on the stage. (direct object, subject)

7. He gave me a smile of encouragement. (indirect object, subject)

8. I nodded to him appreciatively. (direct object, object of a preposition)

PART III   Underline the correct pronoun in parentheses.

9. Gayle and (I, me) are learning some new songs.

10. My brother gave (she, her) and me some sheet music.

11. (He, Him) has high hopes for (us, we).

PART IV   Underline the correct pronouns in parentheses.

12. (She, Her) and (I, me) both play the guitar.

13. Would you come with (she, her) and (I, me) to the performance?

14. (He, Him) and the other musicians will arrive shortly.

PRACTICAL GUIDE TO BETTER ENGLISH

PART V Write the possessive form of each pronoun in parentheses.

15. (you) Did you remember to bring _____ harmonica?

16. (they) Cliff and Raul put _____ jackets in that closet.

17. (we) We have more than thirty songs in _____ repertoire.

PART VI Underline the pronoun in each sentence. On the line, write the noun it refers to.

18. Malvina likes her job.   _____

19. The musicians took their seats.   _____

20. Amanda said that she would play first.   _____

21. Ross picked up his guitar.   _____

PART VII Rewrite this paragraph on the lines below. Replace at least one noun in each sentence with a pronoun.

22–24.

Ross played Ross's favorite tune first. The audience clapped the audience's hands in appreciation. When Gayle saw Ross after the performance, Gayle gave Ross a bouquet.

_____

_____

_____

_____

_____

PART VIII Think about the underlined pronoun in each sentence. Then draw a line under the word in parentheses that tells what kind of pronoun it is.

25. That bass is <u>mine</u>. (possessive, indefinite)

26. <u>Whose</u> drums are these? (possessive, interrogative)

27. <u>I</u> will win a Grammy this year. (indefinite, personal)

28. <u>That</u> is ridiculous! (demonstrative, personal)

PART IX Draw a line under each word that should be capitalized. Add appropriate punctuation.

29. paulo bonito my music teacher was born in brazil on august 8 1970

30. he studied dance music and theater before moving to the united states in june 1992

PRACTICAL GUIDE TO BETTER ENGLISH

UNIT III
Achievement Test, *page 1*

PART I   Read each pair of sentences. Underline each noun in the first sentence. In the second sentence, underline each pronoun that has replaced a noun.

1.   Jane greets customers at the door.
      She greets them at the door.

2.   Matt brings Mrs. Naff a menu.
      He brings her a menu.

3.   Mr. and Mrs. Naff like the desserts.
      They like them.

4.   Wendy bakes baklava in our oven.
      She bakes it in our oven.

PART II   Think about how each underlined pronoun is used in these sentences. Then draw a line under the word or phrase in parentheses that tells how the pronoun is used.

5.   I served 24 parties tonight. (subject, direct object)

6.   A customer asked me for coffee. (direct object, subject)

7.   I quickly brought her a cup. (direct object, indirect object)

8.   She left a generous tip for me. (object of a preposition, subject)

PART III   Underline the correct pronouns in parentheses.

9.   Matt and (I, me) work the evening shift.

10.   The manager lets (he, him) and me eat dinner at the restaurant.

11.   (She, Her) allows (us, we) to order anything on the menu.

PART IV   Underline the correct pronouns in parentheses.

12.   (He, Him) and (I, me) usually have the swordfish.

13.   The chef gives (we, us) and the other employees huge portions.

14.   (Us, We) and our co-workers are quite fond of (he, him).

PART V   Write the possessive form of each pronoun in parentheses.

15.   (I) _____ shift ends at ten o'clock.

16.   (you) Would you like some cheese for _____ pasta?

17.   (they) The Naffs said that _____ salads were delicious.

PRACTICAL GUIDE TO BETTER ENGLISH

PART VI Underline the pronoun in each sentence. On the line, write the noun it refers to.

18. Matt takes off his apron. _____

19. Sabrina counts her tips. _____

20. The Naffs ask for their check. _____

21. Mrs. Morfidis says she will buy more coffee cups. _____

PART VII Rewrite this paragraph on the lines below. Replace at least one noun in each sentence with a pronoun.

22–24.

   Mrs. Morfidis hires good cooks for Mrs. Morfidis's restaurant. On Wednesday Wendy baked Wendy's Chocolate Decadence cake. When the Naffs tasted that cake, the Naffs said it was delicious.

_____

_____

_____

_____

_____

PART VIII Think about the underlined pronoun in each sentence. Then draw a line under the word in parentheses that tells what kind of pronoun it is.

25. Those tips are <u>mine</u>. (possessive, indefinite)

26. <u>Whose</u> apron is that? (demonstrative, interrogative)

27. <u>I</u> have eight tables to wait on. (indefinite, personal)

28. <u>That</u> is too many! (demonstrative, personal)

PART IX Draw a line under each word that should be capitalized. Add appropriate punctuation.

29. anna morfidis my boss was born in athens greece on april 6 1935

30. she worked as a clerk an accountant and a restaurant manager before moving to chicago in may 1995

PRACTICAL GUIDE TO BETTER ENGLISH

UNIT IV
Diagnostic Test, page 1

PART I   Draw a line under each adjective in the following sentences. Do not underline articles. Below each adjective, write the noun it modifies.

1. This small chair is made of the pale wood of a pine.

   _____

2. Those handmade cabinets are the work of patient hands.

   _____

3. Great skill is required to build custom furniture.

   _____

PART II   On the line after each sentence, write the predicate adjective or predicate adjectives that appear in the sentence.

4. Oak is dense and hard.   _____

5. It is plentiful in the United States.   _____

6. Cherrywood looks beautiful with a dark stain.   _____

PART III   Underline each comparative adjective in the sentences below. Circle each superlative adjective.

7. Oak is harder than pine.

8. Many builders believe that redwood is the best wood for construction.

9. Redwood is more resistant to disease than other woods.

PART IV   In the sentences below, draw one line under the verb or verb phrase and draw two lines under the adverb that modifies it.

10. Use that chisel carefully!

11. Martin has expertly carved the design.

12. He skillfully removed the excess wood.

13. Soon his masterpiece will be complete.

PRACTICAL GUIDE TO BETTER ENGLISH

PART V In the sentences below, underline each adverb that modifies an adjective or another adverb. On the first line after the sentence, write the word the adverb modifies. On the second line, tell whether that word is an adjective or an adverb.

14. This is an extremely difficult class. _____ _____

15. She is a very capable woodworker. _____ _____

16. I use this tool most frequently. _____ _____

17. Joel works extremely hard. _____ _____

PART VI Underline each prepositional phrase used as an adjective. Circle each prepositional phrase used as an adverb. On the line, write the noun or verb that is modified.

18. The chisel on the counter is mine. _____

19. People of all ages enjoy carpentry. _____

20. Dierdre works in her studio. _____

21. She sells her work at crafts fairs. _____

PART VII Underline the prepositional phrase in each sentence. Circle each preposition.

22. Dierdre works for herself. _____

23. The instructor of the course is friendly. _____

24. The tools on the table are his. _____

PART VIII Underline the comparative adverbs in the sentences below. Circle the superlative adverbs.

25. No one carves more carefully than Joel.

26. I concentrate better at night than I do during the day.

27. Of all my classmates, Martin works fastest.

PART IX Rewrite the paragraph using correct capitalization and punctuation.

28–30.

   martin puryear is an artist who creates beautiful sculptures from wood he grew up in washington, D.C., and often visited the smithsonian museum of natural history puryear learned woodworking in his father's workshop he also studied art woodworking and sculpture in africa and sweden one of puryear's creations is a series of levers carved from wood

_____

_____

_____

_____

PRACTICAL GUIDE TO BETTER ENGLISH

UNIT IV
Achievement Test, page 1

PART I   Draw a line under each adjective in the following sentences. Do not underline articles. Below each adjective, write the noun it modifies.

1. Purple silk was used to cover the small sofa.

   _____

2. The soft curtains have thin yellow stripes.

   _____

3. This spacious room is decorated with bright fabrics.

   _____

PART II   On the line after each sentence, write the predicate adjective or predicate adjectives that appear in the sentence.

4. Cotton denim is strong.   _____

5. It is durable but soft.   _____

6. Jeans are expensive at department stores.   _____

PART III   Underline each comparative adjective in the sentences below. Circle each superlative adjective.

7. Cotton is softer than wool.

8. However, wool garments offer better protection from the cold.

9. I think that silk is the most luxurious fabric of all.

PART IV   In the sentences below, draw one line under the verb or verb phrase and draw two lines under the adverb that modifies it.

10. Follow the instructions carefully.

11. I have already put them in the dryer.

12. Unfortunately my jeans have shrunk.

13. I have certainly learned my lesson.

PRACTICAL GUIDE TO BETTER ENGLISH

PART V In the sentences below, underline each adverb that modifies an adjective or another adverb. On the first line after the sentence, write the word the adverb modifies. On the second line, tell whether that word is an adjective or an adverb.

14. This is the most expensive laundromat in the city. _____ _____

15. That is a very large washer! _____ _____

16. I recommend this detergent most enthusiastically. _____ _____

17. This dryer works more efficiently than most dryers. _____ _____

PART VI Underline each prepositional phrase used as an adjective. Circle each prepositional phrase used as an adverb. On the line, write the noun or verb that is modified.

18. The laundry in the dryer is mine. _____

19. Please move your basket onto the table. _____

20. The customers at Wishy Washy are rude. _____

21. I'll patronize Launderama in the future. _____

PART VII Underline the prepositional phrase in each sentence. Circle each preposition.

22. The owner of the laundromat is friendly. _____

23. His son works for him. _____

24. They repair the machines on weekdays. _____

PART VIII Underline the comparative adverbs in the sentences below. Circle the superlative adverbs.

25. I think the jumbo-size washer works best.

26. Measure the soap more carefully next time.

27. Your clothes will dry faster in that machine than in this one.

PART IX Rewrite the paragraph using correct capitalization and punctuation.

28–30.

the first washing machines were developed in europe in the early 1800s laundry was placed in a wooden box, to which water had been added the box was tumbled by a hand-operated crank a french inventor named pochon developed a rotating dryer in 1800 the drum rotated over a fire truly automatic washers didn't appear until 1939

_____

_____

_____

_____

PRACTICAL GUIDE TO BETTER ENGLISH

UNIT V
Diagnostic Test, page 1

PART I On the line, write whether the underlined verb is an *action verb* or a *linking verb.*

1. People probably <u>tamed</u> dogs as long ago as 8000 B.C. _____

2. In 1570 Johannes Caius <u>wrote</u> a book about dogs. _____

3. Hundreds of books about dogs <u>are</u> available today. _____

PART II Draw a line under the verb that correctly completes each sentence.

4. Drake's father (run, runs) an obedience school for dogs.

5. Dogs at his school (learn, learns) basic commands.

6. The most important command (is, are) "No!"

7. Owners (praise, praises) their dogs for following commands.

8. Rewards (is, are) an important part of the training.

PART III Underline the verb or verb phrase in each sentence. On the line, write *present*, *past*, or *future* to show when the action takes place.

9. Drake trains particularly stubborn dogs. _____

10. Before training, this dog chewed everything in sight. _____

11. It ignored its owner's commands. _____

12. The dog will be a fine companion someday. _____

PART IV Underline the verb phrase in each sentence. On the line, write *present perfect, past perfect,* or *future perfect* to show the tense form of the verb.

13. Maude has eaten Happy Dog dog food since puppyhood. _____

14. After a year she had grown into a healthy, 50-pound dog. _____

15. By age two she will have gained another ten pounds or so. _____

PART V Underline the verb in each sentence. On the line, write *active* or *passive* to describe the voice of the verb.

16. Australian cattle dogs are used by some ranchers. _____

17. Some ranchers use Australian cattle dogs. _____

18. These tough little dogs nip the heels of cattle. _____

19. The heels of cattle are nipped by these tough little dogs. _____

PART VI In items 20 and 21, write the contraction for each pair of words. Then use each contraction you have written to complete a sentence in items 22 and 23.

20. have not _____

21. you will _____

22. You _____met my dog Roscoe yet.

23. I know _____ like him.

PART VII In each blank, write the appropriate form of the word in parentheses.

24. (be) Roscoe _____ smarter than he looks.

25. (have) He _____ already learned several commands.

26. (take) Yesterday he _____ his final exam at obedience school.

PART VIII Draw a line under each word that should begin with a capital letter. Add necessary punctuation.

27. roscoe my favorite dog was born on july 8 1996

28. he was raised on a puppy farm in san diego california

29. i've traveled with him through california nevada and utah

30. he loves to visit my fathers ranch and he begins barking as soon as he sees its front gate

PRACTICAL GUIDE TO BETTER ENGLISH

UNIT V
Achievement Test, page 1

PART I On the line, write whether the underlined verb is an *action verb* or a *linking verb*.

1. Movies of the early 1900s <u>were</u> silent films. _____

2. In the 1920s engineers <u>created</u> films with recorded sound. _____

3. In 1927 Al Jolson <u>starred</u> in *The Jazz Singer.* _____

PART II Draw a line under the verb that correctly completes each sentence.

4. My sister (like, likes) comedies better than action movies.

5. Do you (think, thinks) this film is exciting?

6. That man behind us (is, are) too talkative.

7. Some people (talk, talks) too loudly in movie theaters.

8. (Do, Does) Andrea have the popcorn?

PART III Underline the verb or verb phrase in each sentence. On the line, write *present*, *past*, or *future* to show when the action takes place.

9. I like this movie. _____

10. It will win some awards next spring. _____

11. The directors chose Vancouver, Canada, as the setting. _____

12. The film crew enjoyed their stay there. _____

PART IV Underline the verb phrase in each sentence. On the line, write *present perfect, past perfect,* or *future perfect* to show the tense form of the verb.

13. My sister has loved movies since preschool.

14. By the end of high school she had made three films of her own.

15. Probably by age 30 she will have directed a wildly successful movie.

PART V Underline the verb in each sentence. On the line, write *active* or *passive* to describe the voice of the verb.

16. *Titanic* has been seen by millions of viewers. _____

17. Millions of viewers have seen *Titanic.* _____

18. Many critics have praised this film. _____

19. This film has been praised by many critics. _____

PRACTICAL GUIDE TO BETTER ENGLISH

PART VI In items 20 and 21, write the contraction for each pair of words. Then use each contraction you have written to complete a sentence in items 22 and 23.

20. I have _____

21. have not _____

22. Dave and Sue still _____ seen that movie.

23. _____ seen it three times.

PART VII In each blank, write the appropriate form of the word in parentheses.

24. (cost) It _____ many millions to make a film like *Titanic*.

25. (be) The sets _____ incredibly expensive to build.

26. (have) The movie studio _____ made huge profits, however.

PART VIII Draw a line under each word that should begin with a capital letter. Add necessary punctuation.

27. my sister directed a film that was first shown on june 7 1999

28. it was filmed in montreal buffalo and rochester

29. that films first scene has become famous but its ending did not win praise

30. her new movie takes place in santa fe new mexico

UNIT VI
Diagnostic Test, page 1

PART I Draw a line under each participle. On the line, write the noun that is modified.

1. This is a borrowed car.   _____

2. Congested traffic annoys me.   _____

3. We passed a vendor selling fresh tacos.   _____

4. My passengers welcomed this unplanned stop.   _____

PART II Combine each pair of sentences into a single sentence by using a participial phrase. You may change other words to make the sentence sound more natural.

5. My car is dented. It needs repair.

   _____

6. Your transmission is leaking. It will cause you trouble.

   _____

PART III Rewrite each sentence so that the participial phrase modifies the appropriate noun.

7. I saw Roger's car walking to school.

   _____

8. I gave a taco to Denise wrapped in foil.

   _____

PART IV Underline each gerund. Then circle the word that tells what kind of sentence element the gerund is.

9. Driving requires patience and skill. (subject, direct object)

10. Mark likes watching the Indy 500. (subject, direct object)

11. Becoming a rally driver is his dream. (subject, object of a preposition)

PART V Circle each gerund. Then underline the entire gerund phrase in each sentence.

12. Driving a race car is a tough job.

13. Making a mistake at high speeds can be deadly.

14. Developing safer automobiles would result in fewer injuries.

PRACTICAL GUIDE TO BETTER ENGLISH

PART VI Underline the infinitive in each sentence.

15. Jan left early to get good seats.

16. The best races to see will be held tomorrow.

17. To argue is pointless.

18. I got permission to attend.

PART VII Circle each infinitive. Draw a line under the entire infinitive phrase.

19. I want to interview the winner.

20. I hope to meet him after the race.

21. He'll probably tell me to study hard.

PART VIII Look at the words in italic type. For items 22 and 23, circle a synonym. For items 24 and 25, circle an antonym.

22.	*superior*	full	worse	supervisor	better
23.	*benefit*	debt	advantage	disgrace	award
24.	*costly*	cheap	perfect	round	forgetful
25.	*rare*	real	plentiful	forceful	kind

PART IX In each blank, write the present-tense form of the verb in parentheses.

26. (look) Jack _____ for good deals on used cars.

27. (read) He and Anna _____ the classified ads every day.

PART X Correct each run-on sentence or comma splice by rewriting it as two sentences. Add words to each fragment to create a complete sentence.

28. Look at this ad, the car sounds terrific.

_____

29. Low mileage and a new radio.

_____

30. Please write down the phone number I'll call the seller.

_____

PRACTICAL GUIDE TO BETTER ENGLISH

UNIT VI
Achievement Test, page 1

PART I Draw a line under each participle. On the line, write the noun that is modified.

1.   We entered the crowded theater.   _____

2.   The woman selling tickets had sold us the last two.   _____

3.   An actor wore polished armor.   _____

4.   A disturbing noise distracted us.   _____

PART II Combine each pair of sentences into a single sentence by using a participial phrase. You may change other words to make the sentence sound more natural.

5.   A baby was crying. She was carried out of the theater.

_____

6.   Leaves had fallen. They covered the sidewalk.

_____

PART III Rewrite each sentence so that the participial phrase modifies the appropriate noun.

7.   I saw a picture of King Kong leaving the theater.

_____

8.   I gave French fries to my sister covered with catsup.

_____

PART IV Underline each gerund. Then circle the word that tells what kind of sentence element the gerund is.

9.   Acting requires talent and training. (subject, direct object)

10.   Becoming a stage actor is Ana's dream. (subject, object of a preposition)

11.   I enjoy reading plays. (subject, direct object)

PART V Circle each gerund. Then underline the entire gerund phrase in each sentence.

12.   Acting in plays can be very exciting.

13.   Overcoming stage fright is not easy.

14.   Rehearsing your lines with a partner may calm your jitters.

PART VI Underline the infinitive in each sentence.

15. I'm anxious to see Ana's new play.

16. The best night to see it is Sunday.

17. To travel together might be wise.

18. Do you want to drive?

PART VII Circle each infinitive. Draw a line under the entire infinitive phrase.

19. I want to meet Ana's director.

20. I hope to meet him after the play.

21. Ana told me to introduce myself.

PART VIII Look at the words in italic type. For items 22 and 23, circle a synonym. For items 24 and 25, circle an antonym.

22.	*innocent*	guilty	blameless	reckless	fearless
23.	*opportunity*	favor	attitude	misfortune	chance
24.	*plentiful*	profuse	scarce	extra	frightening
25.	*calm*	youthful	excellent	nervous	cheap

PART IX In each blank, write the present-tense form of the verb in parentheses.

26. (perform) Ana sometimes _____ in plays by Shakespeare.

27. (see) Millie and I _____ her shows whenever we can.

PART X Correct each run-on sentence or comma splice by rewriting it as two sentences. Add words to each fragment to create a complete sentence.

28. Shakespeare wrote several plays about historical figures, *Henry VIII* is one of them.

_____

29. *Romeo and Juliet*, a tragic story.

_____

30. Two young people fall in love their families bitterly oppose the relationship.

_____

Name_____   Date _____

UNIT VII
Diagnostic Test, page 1

PART I Circle the introductory word in each dependent clause. Underline the entire dependent clause.

1. Because of their great size, manatees look threatening.

2. Although manatees are huge, they are harmless.

3. I saw a manatee when I visited Florida.

4. They are shy, gentle creatures that are also endangered.

PART II Write a complex sentence by making a dependent clause of one sentence. Use the word in parentheses as the introductory word of the clause.

5. (as) Our boat approached the manatee. It dove deep into the river.

    _____

6. (because) Many manatees bear scars. Boat propellers have nicked them.

    _____

7. (after) The manatee resurfaced. Our boat left.

    _____

8. (when) We spotted a flamingo. We were thrilled.

    _____

PART III Underline each dependent clause. Draw a box around the word it modifies.

9. The alligator is the creature that rules Florida's swamps.

10. These reptiles, which are plentiful in Florida, are vicious predators.

PART IV Use *who, which,* or *that* to complete each sentence.

11. A person _____ traps alligators for a living must be courageous and skilled.

12. An alligator _____ invades backyards must be caught and moved.

PART V Put a comma after each adverb clause that comes at the beginning of a sentence. Underline each adverb clause that does not.

13. When a pet alligator was released in a city pond nearby residents were alarmed.

14. The alligator became dangerous when it grew to four feet in length.

15. After the hunter trapped the creature he released it into the wild.

16. This incident shows why alligator hunters are needed.

PRACTICAL GUIDE TO BETTER ENGLISH

PART VI Write a compound sentence by combining the two short sentences with the word in parentheses.

17. My grandfather plays tennis. He skis down the steepest mountains.

(and) _____

18. We could play singles. We could enter the doubles tournament.

(or) _____

PART VII First, write a compound sentence by joining each pair of short sentences with the coordinating conjunction indicated. Then rewrite each compound sentence as a complex sentence. Use the word in parentheses to begin the dependent clause.

19. Mrs. Dawson has a mean serve. My grandmother can beat her.

(but) _____

(although) _____

20. The Dawsons have exercised all their lives. They are in good shape.

(and) _____

(because) _____

PART VIII Cross out the unnecessary word or words in each sentence.

21. Where is my tennis racket at?

22. Mr. Dawson he has like challenged me to a game.

23. That there net keeps blocking my serves.

PART IX Draw a line through any misspelled word in the paragraph below, and write the correct spelling above it.

24–27.

Florida is a grate place for peeple who love the outdours. It's climate is cumfortible throughout the year. Tenis, diveing, swiming, and golf are populer sports. Wildlife enthusiasts visit Florida to study fish and birds. More spesies of fish live in Florida's waterways than in any other part of the world.

PART X Rewrite each sentence to correct the use of double negatives.

28. Humid weather don't bother me none.

_____

29. Alicia didn't bring no sunscreen.

_____

30. Don't never swim alone.

_____

PRACTICAL GUIDE TO BETTER ENGLISH

UNIT VII
Achievement Test, page 1

PART I Circle the introductory word in each dependent clause. Underline the entire dependent clause.

1. Few animals eat cactuses because they have spines.

2. If you hear a dry rattling sound, you should beware.

3. Rattlers usually warn enemies before they strike.

4. Although they are notorious for their foul odor, skunks are beautiful creatures.

PART II Write a complex sentence by making a dependent clause of one sentence. Use the word in parentheses as the introductory word of the clause.

5. (as) I approached the skunk. It stamped its front feet.

   _____

6. (because) It warned me. I avoided a very unpleasant experience.

   _____

7. (after) An animal encounters a skunk. That animal never forgets it.

   _____

8. (when) That animal sees a skunk. It flees.

   _____

PART III Underline each dependent clause. Draw a box around the word it modifies.

9. Another creature that has distinctive markings is the black widow.

10. The female, which has a red or yellow mark on its abdomen, is poisonous.

PART IV Use *who*, *which*, or *that* to complete each sentence.

11. Someone _____ has been bitten by a black widow may grow very ill.

12. Females sometimes kill their mates, _____ explains this spider's name.

PART V Put a comma after each adverb clause that comes at the beginning of a sentence. Underline each adverb clause that does not.

13. Hikers should be cautious when exploring the backwoods.

14. If you see a black widow don't go near it!

15. Although these spiders are most common in the South, they live throughout the United States.

16. You can safely enjoy the outdoors if you use appropriate caution.

PRACTICAL GUIDE TO BETTER ENGLISH

PART VI Write a compound sentence by combining the two short sentences with the word in parentheses.

17. The porcupine whacked the hound with its tail. The dog howled in pain.

    (and) _____

18. A porcupine cannot shoot its quills. It can release them on contact with an attacker.

    (but) _____

PART VII First, write a compound sentence by joining each pair of short sentences with the coordinating conjunction indicated. Then rewrite each compound sentence as a complex sentence. Use the word in parentheses to begin the dependent clause.

19. Hedgehogs also have quills. They are sometimes mistaken for porcupines.

    (and) _____

    (because) _____

20. Porcupines have soft bellies. Predators often flip them onto their backs.

    (and) _____

    (since) _____

PART VIII Cross out the unnecessary word or words in each sentence.

21. Where did that there hedgehog go to?

22. The porcupine it disappeared into a ravine.

23. It like waddles when it walks.

PART IX Draw a line through any misspelled word in the paragraph below, and write the correct spelling above it.

24–27.

   "Wonders of the Wild" is a grate show for nature lovers. It has been on public telivision for foreteen years. The narrator, Jack Greenwood, seems to love teaching veiwers about plants and anamels. He is especially intrested in the creatures of South America's rain forrest. I loved his speshul report on tropicle birds.

PART X Rewrite each sentence to correct the use of double negatives.

28. Don't never annoy a skunk.

    _____

29. I've never seen no black widows in my yard.

    _____

30. I didn't bring no snake bite kit with me.

    _____

PRACTICAL GUIDE TO BETTER ENGLISH

UNIT VIII
Diagnostic Test, *page 1*

PART I Write a business letter to the Personnel Manager of Bay Stadium, Box 4468, Santa Rosa, California 95405. Ask that person to send you a job application for summer job positions at the stadium. Use your own name and address in the heading.

1–6.   _____

_____

_____

_____

_____

_____

_____

_____

_____

PART II Address an envelope for the letter you wrote. Use abbreviations wherever you can. Use your own address as the return address.

7–12.

PRACTICAL GUIDE TO BETTER ENGLISH

PART III Read the following advertisement for a job. Then write what each boldfaced word means.

Cooks Needed—**exp. pref.**

F/T and **P/T**

Busy downtown restaurant needs help with afternoon/eve. shift. Immed. openings. Call 424-2910—Ms. Ryan   **EOE**

13.   F/T _____

14.   P/T _____

15.   exp. pref. _____

PART IV Find the answers to these questions in the Handbook Guide, which begins on page 113. Then fill in each blank to complete the sentence.

16.   An _____ sentence is a sentence that asks something.

17.   A prepositional phrase begins with a _____.

18.   A gerund is the present participle of a verb used as a _____.

PART V Draw a line under the word that correctly completes each sentence.

19.   (Whose, Who's) applying for the position of assistant coach?

20.   I'm afraid (its, it's) been filled already.

21.   We had to choose (between, among) you and one other candidate.

22.   (There, Their) are many other jobs available, however.

PART VI Draw a line under the word that correctly completes each sentence.

23.   Please (sit, set) that application on the desk.

24.   You can (lie, lay) it next to the others.

25.   I hope I don't (lay, lie) awake all night wondering if I got the job.

PART VII First put these words in alphabetical order. Then look up each word in the dictionary. Use hyphens to divide the words into syllables.

pursuit	26.	_____	_____
environment	27.	_____	_____
putter	28.	_____	_____

PART VIII Use a dictionary to find out whether each statement is true or false. Write *true* or *false* on the line.

29.   You could order a *pipette* for dinner.   _____

30.   *Knell* has the same beginning sound as *canal*   _____

Name_____   Date _____

UNIT VIII
Achievement Test, page 1

PART I   Write a business letter to Anna Morfidis, Anna's Cafe, Box 1126, Redmond, Washington 98052. Ask Mrs. Morfidis to send you a job application for summer job positions at her restaurant. Use your own name and address in the heading.

1–6.   _____

_____

_____

_____

_____

_____

_____

_____

_____

_____

PART II   Address an envelope for the letter you wrote. Use abbreviations wherever you can. Use your own address as the return address.

7–12.

PRACTICAL GUIDE TO BETTER ENGLISH

PART III Read the following advertisement for a job. Then write what each boldfaced word means.

Sales Assistant
F/T and **P/T** positions
Shoe store in mall has immediate openings.
exp. pref.
Call Mr. Atkins at 989-7200   **EOE**

13.   F/T _____

14.   P/T _____

15.   exp. pref. _____

PART IV Find the answers to these questions in the Handbook Guide, which begins on page 113. Then fill in each blank to complete the sentence.

16.   The words *and, but,* and *or* are called _____.

17.   An infinitive phrase begins with the word _____.

18.   The four words used as demonstrative pronouns are _____, _____, _____, and _____.

PART V Draw a line under the word that correctly completes each sentence.

19.   It's hard to choose (between, among) the lasagne and the meatloaf.

20.   (Who's, Whose) chocolate truffle is this?

21.   (Its, It's) center is filled with raspberry fudge.

22.   (There, Their) are so many wonderful dishes to choose from.

PART VI Draw a line under the word that correctly completes each sentence.

23.   Please (sit, set) those glasses on the tray.

24.   You can (lie, lay) those towels on the counter.

25.   I'll have to (lay, lie) down after this meal!

PART VII First put these words in alphabetical order. Then look up each word in the dictionary. Use hyphens to divide the words into syllables.

supper   26.   _____   _____

exclamation   27.   _____   _____

surround   28.   _____   _____

PART VIII Use a dictionary to find out whether each statement is true or false. Write *true* or *false* on the line.

29.   You *exult* if you feel happy and triumphant.   _____

30.   The first syllable of *conic* is pronounced like *coal*.   _____

PRACTICAL GUIDE TO BETTER ENGLISH

Answer Keys—Diagnostic Tests

UNIT I

1. .
2. F
3. .
4. F
5. ? interrogative
6. ! exclamatory
7. . imperative
8. . declarative
9. wind, controls, direction
10. pilot, controls, movement
11. Will, has taken, pictures
12. She is an industrious <u>woman</u>.
13. He is very (artistic)
14. That was a terrible <u>movie</u>.
15. Alison gave me the (tickets). (me)
16. Will told his sister a scary (story) (sister)
17. A farmer sold Paul some ripe (tomatoes). (Paul)
18. That <u>balloon</u> <u>is</u> particularly [colorful].
19. <u>Mr. Pritchard</u> <u>has owned</u> the (company) for six years.
20. The company's best <u>pilot</u> <u>is</u> a [woman] from Iowa.
21. doesn't   22. Are   23. Isn't
24. <u>i've</u> scheduled our balloon trip for <u>sunday</u>, <u>may</u> 16.
25. <u>our</u> guide, <u>mr.</u> <u>pritchard</u>, is from <u>aberdeen</u>, <u>scotland</u>.
26. <u>his</u> company is called <u>limitless</u> <u>sky</u> <u>adventures</u>.
27. <u>they</u> have offices in <u>albuquerque</u>, <u>topeka</u>, and <u>stillwater</u>.
28. "Napa, California, is famous for ballooning," explained Rick.
29. "Rick, have you ever flown a balloon?" asked Suzanne.
30. Rick replied, "Yes, I've ballooned in Utah, Nevada, and Kansas."

UNIT II

1. simple
2. <u>It was once a tall, pointed mountain</u>, (but) <u>volcanic activity changed its shape</u>. (compound)
3. simple
4. <u>The mountain rumbled for months</u>, (and) <u>finally the top blew off</u>. (compound)
5. Scientists expected an eruption, but its suddenness surprised them.
6. A rumbling sound filled the air, and ash poured into the sky.
7. We could view photographs of the event, or we could watch a videotape.
8. Trees were incinerated, and animal habitats were destroyed.
9. The mountain spewed ash and belched smoke.
10. Scientists witnessed the eruption and studied its effects.
11. Is that a bird or a plane?
12. Did André take your coat and offer you some lemonade?
13. The lemonade is cold and delicious.
14. Did lava cover the mountainsides, or were some patches left unharmed?
15. Trees, homes, and roads were instantly destroyed.
16. Local residents had some warning, luckily, and took precautions.
17. How awful the destruction was!
18-21. Answers will vary. Forms are listed below.
18. men   19. ponies   20. women's   21. cars'
22. the girls' shoes   24.   the butcher's sausages
23. the band's songs
25. The <u>landscape</u> was a desolate <u>sight</u>. (subject, predicate noun)

26. <u>Ash</u> covered the <u>fields</u>. (subject, direct object)
27. <u>Dawn</u> gave the <u>land</u> an eerie <u>glow</u>. (subject, indirect object, direct object)
28-30.   <u>after</u> a few years, signs of life began to return to <u>mt. st. helens</u>. <u>seedlings</u> poked up through the ash. <u>deer</u>, squirrels, and foxes began to return. <u>the people of washington</u> must have been quite relieved that the lifeless state was not permanent. <u>homes</u> have not been built near the blast zone, however. <u>scientists</u> believe that <u>mt. st. helens</u> will erupt again sometime in the future.

UNIT III

1. <u>Gayle</u> bought a <u>violin</u>. <u>She</u> bought <u>it</u>.
2. The <u>guitars</u> are made of <u>rosewood</u>. <u>They</u> are made of rosewood.
3. Many <u>musicians</u> practice <u>scales</u> regularly. <u>They</u> practice <u>them</u> regularly.
4. <u>Raul</u> is learning to play the <u>piano</u>. <u>He</u> is learning to play <u>it</u>.
5. subject
6. direct object
7. indirect object
8. object of a preposition
9. I
10. her
11. He, us
12. She, I
13. her, me
14. He
15. your
16. their
17. our
18. her, Malvina
19. their, musicians
20. she, Amanda
21. his, Ross
22-24. Answers may vary. Ross played his favorite tune first. The audience clapped their hands in appreciation. When Gayle saw Ross after the performance, she gave him a bouquet.
25. possessive
26. interrogative
27. personal
28. demonstrative
29. <u>paulo</u> <u>bonito</u>, my music teacher, was born in <u>brazil</u> on <u>august</u> 8, 1970.
30. <u>he</u> studied dance, music, and theater before moving to the <u>united</u> <u>states</u> in <u>june</u> 1992.

UNIT IV

1. This <u>small</u> chair is made of the <u>pale</u> wood of a pine. (chair, wood)
2. Those <u>handmade</u> cabinets are the work of <u>patient</u> hands. (cabinets, hands)
3. <u>Great</u> skill is required to build <u>custom</u> furniture. (skill, furniture)
4. dense, hard   5. plentiful   6. beautiful
7. Oak is <u>harder</u> than pine.
8. Many builders believe that redwood is the (best) wood for construction.
9. Redwood is <u>more</u> <u>resistant</u> to disease than other woods.
10. <u>Use</u> that chisel <u>carefully</u>!
11. Martin <u>has</u> <u>expertly</u> <u>carved</u> the design.
12. He <u>skillfully</u> <u>removed</u> the excess wood.
13. <u>Soon</u> his masterpiece <u>will be</u> complete.
14. This is an <u>extremely</u> difficult class. (difficult, adjective)
15. She is a <u>very</u> capable woodworker. (capable, adjective)
16. I use this tool <u>most</u> frequently. (frequently, adverb)
17. Joel works <u>extremely</u> hard. (hard, adverb)
18. The chisel <u>on the counter</u> is mine. (chisel)
19. People <u>of all ages</u> enjoy carpentry. (people)
20. Diedre works (in her studio) (works)
21. She sells her work (at crafts fairs) (sells)
22. Diedre works (for herself)
23. The instructor (of the course) is friendly.
24. The tools (on the table) are his.

25. No one carves <u>more carefully</u> than Joel.
26. I concentrate <u>better</u> at night than I do <u>during</u> the day.
27. Of all my classmates, Martin works (fastest).
28-30. Martin Puryear is an artist who creates beautiful sculptures from wood. He grew up in Washington, D.C., and often visited the Smithsonian Museum of Natural History. Puryear learned woodworking in his father's workshop. He also studied art, woodworking, and sculpture in Africa and Sweden. One of Puryear's creations is a series of levers carved from wood.

UNIT V

1. action 3. linking 5. learn 7. praise
2. action 4. runs 6. is 8. are
9. trains, present 11. ignored, past
10. chewed, past 12. will be, future
13. has eaten, present perfect
14. had grown, past perfect
15. will have gained, future perfect
16. are used, passive 18. nip, active
17. use, active 19. are nipped, passive
20. haven't 22. haven't 24. is 26. took
21. you'll 23. you'll 25. has
27. <u>roscoe</u>, my favorite dog, was born on <u>july</u> 8, 1996.
28. <u>he</u> was raised on a puppy farm in <u>san diego</u>, <u>california</u>.
29. <u>i've</u> traveled with him through <u>california</u>, <u>nevada</u>, and <u>utah</u>.
30. <u>he</u> loves to visit my father's ranch, and he begins barking as soon as he sees its front gate.

UNIT VI

1. This is a <u>borrowed</u> car. (car)
2. <u>Congested</u> traffic annoys me. (traffic)
3. We passed a vendor <u>selling</u> fresh tacos. (vendor)
4. My passengers welcomed this <u>unplanned</u> stop. (stop)
For items 5–8, answers may vary.
5. My dented car needs repair.
6. Your leaking transmission will cause you trouble.
7. Walking to school, I saw Roger's car.
8. I gave Denise a taco wrapped in foil.
9. Driving, subject 11. becoming, subject
10. watching, direct object 12. (Driving) a race car
13. (Making) a mistake at high speeds
14. (Developing) safer automobiles
15. <u>to get</u> 16. <u>to see</u> 17. <u>To argue</u> 18. <u>to attend</u>
19. I want (to interview) the winner.
20. I hope (to meet) him after the race.
21. He'll probably tell me (to study) hard.
22. better 24. cheap 26. looks
23. advantage 25. plentiful 27. read
Answers may vary for items 28-30.
28. Look at this ad. The car sounds terrific.
29. The car has low mileage. It also has a new radio.
30. Please write down the phone number for me. I'll call the seller as soon as I can.

UNIT VII

1. (Because) of their great size, manatees look threatening.
2. (Although) manatees are huge, they are harmless.
3. I saw a manatee (when) I visited Florida.
4. They are shy, gentle creatures (that) are also endangered.
5. As our boat approached the manatee, it dove deep into the river.

6. Because boat propellers have nicked them, many manatees bear scars.
7. After our boat left, the manatee resurfaced.
8. When we spotted a flamingo, we were thrilled.
9. The alligator is the [creature] that rules Florida's swamps.
10. These [reptiles], which are plentiful in Florida, are vicious predators.
11. who 12. that
13. When a pet alligator was released in a city pond, nearby residents were alarmed.
14. The alligator became dangerous <u>when it grew to four feet in length</u>.
15. After the hunter trapped the creature, he released it into the wild.
16. This incident shows <u>why alligator hunters are needed</u>.
17. My grandfather plays tennis, and he skis down the steepest mountains.
18. We could play singles, or we could enter the doubles tournament.
19. Mrs. Dawson has a mean serve, but my grandmother can beat her.
Although Mrs. Dawson has a mean serve, my grandmother can beat her.
20. The Dawsons have exercised all their lives, and they are in good shape.
Because the Dawsons have exercised all their lives, they are in good shape.
21. at 22. he, like 23. there
24-27. great, people, outdoors, Its, comfortable, Tennis, diving, swimming, popular, species
For items 28–30, answers may vary.
28. Humid weather doesn't bother me.
29. Alicia didn't bring any sunscreen.
30. Don't ever swim alone.

UNIT VIII

1-6. Answers may vary.   <student's address>
<today's date>

Personnel Manager
Bay Stadium
Box 4468
Santa Rosa, CA 95405

Dear Personnel Manager:

Please send me a job application for summer job positions at the stadium. Thank you for your time.

Sincerely yours,
<student's signature>
7-12. <Student's address should be at upper left.>
Personnel Manager
Bay Stadium
Box 4468
Santa Rosa, CA 95405
13. full-time 14. part-time
15. experience preferred 16. interrogative
17. preposition 19. Who's 21. between 23. set
18. noun 20. it's 22. There 24. lay
25. lie 26. environment, en-vi-ron-ment
27. pursuit, pur-suit 28. putter, put-ter (*also* putt-er)
29. false
30. false

Answer Keys—Achievement Tests

UNIT I

1. .   2. F   3. F   4. .
5. . imperative   8. ! exclamatory
6. ? interrogative   9. Echidnas, lay, eggs
7. . declarative   10. mammals, eat, ants
11. spines, discourage, attackers
12. You are a clever <u>person</u>.   13. That is a valuable <u>ring</u>.
14. Your apartment is quite (large).
15. Raquel sent me a (postcard) from Australia. (me)
16. The Koala fed her baby some (leaves). (baby)
17. I bought my grandmother some (roses). (grandmother)
18. <u>Marsupials</u> <u>are</u> remarkable [creatures].
19. <u>I</u> <u>have been studying</u> Australian (wildlife) for a year.
20. The <u>platypus</u> <u>is</u> [unique] among mammals.
21. Isn't   22. Are   23. thinks
24. <u>on</u> <u>sunday</u>, <u>march</u> 29, we watched a show at the <u>international</u> <u>academy</u> of <u>science</u>.
25. <u>the</u> narrator was <u>dr.</u> <u>angela</u> <u>warren</u> from <u>sydney</u>, <u>australia</u>.
26. <u>some</u> <u>australian</u> species are also native to <u>new</u> <u>guinea</u>.
27. <u>dr.</u> <u>warren</u> has attended conferences in <u>north</u> <u>america</u>, <u>australia</u>, and <u>south</u> <u>america</u>.
28. "Sydney, Australia, is situated on a large, deep, beautiful harbor," said Jack.
29. "Jack, don't the people of Sydney have an unusual nickname?" asked Wanda.
30. Jack replied, "Yes, the residents of Sydney are called *Sydneysiders*."

UNIT II

1. simple
2. <u>The queen lays eggs</u>, (and) <u>workers keep the colony running</u>. (compound)
3. simple
4. <u>Most ants are a dull color</u>, (but) <u>some are colorful</u>. (compound)
5. Male ants are larger than workers, but they are smaller than queens.
6. That could be a harvester ant, or it could be a weaver ant.
7. Ants are social, and they are loyal to their colony.
8. Army ants march in swarms and eat any insects in their path.
9. Male ants and queens have wings.
10. Ants' nests have many tunnels and chambers.
11. Is an anthill more like a beehive or a spider nest?
12. Workers build the nest and care for the young.
13. Soldier ants are large and fierce.
14. Are there ants in the cupboard again, or are you shrieking about something else?
15. This time they're in the honey, the sugar, and the cereal.
16. Ants love those foods, of course, and anything else sweet.
17. What a mess this is!
18-21. Answers may vary. Items to be included are listed below.
18. mice   19. butterflies   20. children's   21. ants'
22. the ants' nest   23. the family's sandwiches
24. the insects' trail
25. A <u>soldier</u> gave her <u>enemy</u> a <u>shove</u>. (subject, indirect object, direct object)
26. The <u>ant</u> was defending her <u>colony</u>. (subject, direct object)
27. Some <u>ants</u> are ferocious <u>fighters</u>. (subject, predicate noun)
28-30.   <u>leaf-cutter</u> ants live in parts of <u>south</u> <u>america</u>. <u>they</u> cut pieces of leaves, carry them to their nest,

and chew them into pulp. <u>the</u> ants use this pulp to fertilize fungus gardens. <u>the</u> fungi produce tiny knobs, which the ants eat. <u>brazilian</u> <u>leaf-cutter</u> ants are considered pests because they strip leaves from orange trees and other crops.

UNIT III

1. <u>Jane</u> greets <u>customers</u> at the <u>door</u>. <u>She</u> greets <u>them</u> at the door.
2. <u>Matt</u> brings <u>Mrs.</u> <u>Naff</u> a <u>menu</u>. <u>He</u> brings <u>her</u> a menu.
3. <u>Mr.</u> and <u>Mrs.</u> <u>Naff</u> like the <u>desserts</u>. <u>They</u> like <u>them</u>.
4. <u>Wendy</u> bakes <u>baklava</u> in our <u>oven</u>. <u>She</u> bakes <u>it</u> in our oven.
5. subject   6. direct object   7. indirect object
8. object of a preposition
9. I   13. us   17. their
10. him   14. We, him   18. his, Matt
11. She, us   15. My   19. her, Sabrina
12. He, I   16. your
20. their, The Naffs   21. she, Mrs. Morfidis
22-24. Answers may vary. Mrs. Morfidis hires good cooks for her restaurant. On Wednesday Wendy baked her Chocolate Decadence cake. When the Naffs tasted that cake, they said it was delicious.
25. possessive   27. personal
26. interrogative   28. demonstrative
29. <u>anna</u> <u>morfidis</u>, my boss, was born in <u>athens</u>, <u>greece</u>, on <u>april</u> 6, 1935.
30. <u>she</u> worked as a clerk, an accountant, and a restaurant manager before moving to <u>chicago</u> in <u>may</u> 1995.

UNIT IV

1. <u>Purple</u> silk was used to cover the <u>small</u> sofa. (silk, sofa)
2. The <u>soft</u> curtains have <u>thin</u> <u>yellow</u> stripes. (curtains, stripes, stripes)
3. This <u>spacious</u> room is decorated with <u>bright</u> fabrics. (room, fabrics)
4. strong   5. durable, soft   6. expensive
7. Cotton is <u>softer</u> than wool.
8. However, wool garments offer <u>better</u> protection from the cold.
9. I think that silk is the (most luxurious) fabric of all.
10. <u>Follow</u> the instructions <u>carefully</u>.
11. I <u>have</u> <u>already</u> <u>put</u> them in the dryer.
12. <u>Unfortunately</u> my jeans <u>have shrunk</u>.
13. I <u>have</u> <u>certainly</u> <u>learned</u> my lesson.
14. This is the <u>most</u> expensive laundromat in the city. (expensive, adjective)
15. That is a <u>very</u> large washer! (large, adjective)
16. I recommend this detergent <u>most</u> enthusiastically. (enthusiastically, adverb)
17. This dryer works <u>more</u> efficiently than most dryers. (efficiently, adverb)
18. The laundry <u>in the dryer</u> is mine. (laundry)
19. Please move your basket (onto the table) (move)
20. The customers <u>at Wishy Washy</u> are rude. (customers)
21. I'll patronize Launderama (in the future) (patronize)
22. The owner (of) the laundromat is friendly.
23. His son works (for him).
24. They repair the machines (on) weekdays.
25. I think the jumbo-size washer works (best).
26. Measure the soap <u>more carefully</u> next time.
27. Your clothes will dry <u>faster</u> in that machine than in this one.

28-30. the first washing machines were developed in europe in the early 1800s. laundry was placed in a wooden box, to which water had been added. the box was tumbled by a hand-operated crank. a french inventor named pochon developed a rotating dryer in 1800. the drum rotated over a fire. truly automatic washers didn't appear until 1939.

UNIT V

1. linking   3. action   5. think   7. talk
2. action   4. likes   6. is   8. Does
9. like, present   12. enjoyed, past
10. will win, future   13. has loved, present perfect
11. chose, past   14. had made, past perfect
15. will have directed, future perfect
16. has been seen, passive   18. have praised, active
17. have seen, active   19. has been praised, passive
20. I've   22. haven't   24. costs   26. has
21. haven't   23. I've   25. are
27. my sister directed a film that was first shown on june 7, 1999.
28. it was filmed in montreal, buffalo, and rochester.
29. that film's first scene has become famous, but its ending did not win praise.
30. her new movie takes place in santa fe, new mexico.

UNIT VI

1. crowded, theater   3. polished, armor
2. selling, woman   4. disturbing, noise
For items 5–8, answers may vary.
5. A crying baby was carried out of the theater.
6. Fallen leaves covered the sidewalk.
7. Leaving the theater, I saw a picture of King Kong.
8. I gave my sister French fries covered with catsup.
9. Acting requires talent and training. (subject)
10. Becoming a stage actor is Ana's dream. (subject)
11. I enjoy reading plays. (direct object)
12. Acting in plays can be very exciting.
13. Overcoming stage fright is not easy.
14. Rehearsing your lines with a partner may calm your jitters.
15. I'm anxious to see Ana's new play.
16. The best night to see it is Sunday.
17. To travel together might be wise.
18. Do you want to drive?
19. I want to meet Ana's director.
20. I hope to meet him after the play.
21. Ana told me to introduce myself.
22. blameless   24. scarce   26. performs
23. chance   25. nervous   27. see
Answers may vary for items 28-30.
28. Shakespeare wrote several plays about historical figures. *Henry VIII* is one of those plays.
29. *Romeo and Juliet* was also written by Shakespeare. It is a tragic story.
30. In the play, two young people fall in love. Their families bitterly oppose the relationship, however.

UNIT VII

1. Few animals eat cactuses because they have spines.
2. If you hear a dry rattling sound, you should beware.
3. Rattlers usually warn enemies before they strike.
4. Although they are notorious for their foul odor, skunks are beautiful creatures.
5. As I approached the skunk, it stamped its front feet.

6. Because it warned me, I avoided a very unpleasant experience.
7. After an animal encounters a skunk, that animal never forgets it.
8. When that animal sees a skunk, it flees.
9. Another creature that has distinctive markings is the black widow.
10. The female, which has a red or yellow mark on its abdomen, is poisonous.
11. who   12. which
13. Hikers should be cautious when exploring the backwoods.
14. If you see a black widow, don't go near it!
15. Although these spiders are most common in the South, they live throughout the United States.
16. You can safely enjoy the outdoors if you use appropriate caution.
17. The porcupine whacked the hound with its tail, and the dog howled in pain.
18. A porcupine cannot shoot its quills, but it can release them on contact with an attacker.
19. Hedgehogs also have quills, and they are sometimes mistaken for porcupines.
Because hedgehogs also have quills, they are sometimes mistaken for porcupines.
20. Porcupines have soft bellies, and predators often flip them onto their backs.
Since porcupines have soft bellies, predators often flip them onto their backs.
21. there, to   22. it   23. like
24-27. great, television, fourteen, viewers, animals, especially, interested, forest, special, tropical
For items 34–36, answers may vary.
28. Don't ever annoy a skunk.
29. I've never seen any black widows in my yard.
30. I didn't bring a snake bite kit with me.

UNIT VIII

1-6. Answers may vary.   <student's address>
                           <today's date>

Anna Morfidis
Anna's Cafe
Box 1126
Redmond, WA 98052

Dear Mrs. Morfidis:

Please send me a job application for summer job positions at your restaurant. Thank you for your time.
                     Sincerely yours,
                     <student's signature>

7-12. <student's address>
                   Mrs. Anna Morfidis
                   Anna's Cafe
                   Box 1126
                   Redmond, WA 98052
13. full-time   16. conjunctions
14. part-time   17. to
15. experience preferred   18. this, that, these, those
19. between   21. Its   23. set   25. lie
20. Whose   22. There   24. lay
26. exclamation, ex-cla-ma-tion   29. true
27. supper, sup-per   30. false
28. surround, sur-round

Individual Record-Keeping Form

Student's Name _____

DIAGNOSTIC AND ACHIEVEMENT TESTS

	DIAGNOSTIC (Perfect Score: 30)	ACHIEVEMENT (Perfect Score: 30)	OBSERVATIONS
Unit I			
Unit II			
Unit III			
Unit IV			
Unit V			
Unit VI			
Unit VII			
Unit VIII			

Overall Assessment: _____

_____

_____

ORAL LANGUAGE OBSERVATION CHECKLIST

Listening   (Observe student's ability to: follow oral directions; understand passages read aloud; respond to questions; retain information presented orally.)

Date   *Task*   *Observation*

_____   _____   _____

_____   _____   _____

_____   _____   _____

_____   _____   _____

Speaking   (Observe student's ability to: use correct syntax; use standard English when appropriate; explain ideas or processes; summarize new concepts; retell stories.)

Date   *Task*   *Observation*

_____   _____   _____

_____   _____   _____

_____   _____   _____

_____   _____   _____

Overall Assessment: _____

_____

_____

Writing Rubric and Evaluation Checklists

Using the Writing Rubric. This rubric summarizes general characteristics of compositions written by students of varying levels of proficiency. Use this rubric in conjunction with the Checklists for Evaluating Composition Lessons, which appear on the next four pages, to help you evaluate students' writing.

Superior (4)

- Purpose, task, and audience (if specified) are addressed.
- Composition structure shows an understanding of the structure of the writing form.
- Ideas are well organized and elaborated upon in detail.
- Sentences are complete and correctly written.
- Capitalization and punctuation are used correctly.
- Nearly all words are spelled correctly.

Good (3)

- Purpose, task, and audience (if specified) are addressed fairly effectively.
- Composition structure shows some sense of the structure of the writing form.
- Ideas are organized, but not elaborated upon; or, writing exhibits good use of elaboration and detail, but ideas are not clearly organized.
- Most sentences are complete and correctly written.
- Most capitalization and punctuation are used correctly.
- Most words are spelled correctly.

Average (2)

- Task, purpose, and audience (if specified) are addressed to some extent.
- Organization of ideas is not apparent; little elaboration or detail is used.
- Shows some understanding of the structure of the writing form, but may have omitted key elements (such as a topic sentence or a conclusion).
- Writing may lack unity and focus; may contain nonsequiturs or sentences off the topic.
- Some fragments, run-ons, or comma splices may appear.
- Structure of some sentences is awkward or simplistic.
- A number of errors in capitalization, punctuation, and spelling occur.

Working Toward Improvement (1)

- Task, purpose, and audience (if specified) are not addressed.
- Writing lacks organization and focus: sentences may ramble; ideas seem unconnected; some sentences do not address topic.
- Writing shows little or no understanding of the structure or purpose of the writing form.
- Writing shows limited or no awareness of paragraph structure.
- Writing shows limited control of language; many sentences are incomplete or improperly structured.
- Writing contains many errors in grammar, usage, mechanics, and spelling.

Using the Evaluation Checklists. Duplicate a set of checklists for each student. Use them to assist you in evaluating each student's written work over the course of the year. To evaluate each writing lesson, check the box next to each item the student has completed correctly. Then add the check marks and record the score on the line. In addition to this score, give each writing assignment an overall score based on the Writing Rubric.

Checklists for Evaluating Composition Lessons

Student's Name_____

Use check marks to indicate items answered correctly and objectives fulfilled.

LESSON 10: Writing a Descriptive Essay

Read a Descriptive Essay

Item   *Correct Response*
- ❏ 1.   a schoolyard
- ❏ 2.   The X should be by the first paragraph; the star should be by the last paragraph.
- ❏ 3.   because the writer is describing two separate time periods
- ❏ 4.   Possible responses: **sight**—*Puddles of children;* **smell**—*The smell of half-eaten sandwiches and orange peels;* **sound**—*they shriek with delight*
- ❏ 5.   Responses will vary. (Possible response: *A giant ship painted in royal blues and persimmon reds is ready to set sail over the sea of children.*)

Write a Descriptive Essay Check whether the student has
- ❏ selected an appropriate topic and appropriate time periods.
- ❏ identified details that appeal to the senses. (Review the chart students completed. Some topics may only lend themselves to two or three types of sensory descriptions.)
- ❏ revised the paragraph. (Review the first draft and have the student explain how it was revised.)

Evaluating the Description Check whether the student has
- ❏ understood the purpose of a descriptive essay.
- ❏ introduced the topic in the first paragraph.
- ❏ begun each paragraph with a topic sentence.
- ❏ used a separate paragraph for each time period.
- ❏ summarized his or her ideas in the last paragraph.
- ❏ used colorful words and phrases that appeal to the senses.
- ❏ used complete sentences.
- ❏ used correct capitalization and punctuation.
- ❏ displayed the use of original language.

Perfect Score: 17 Student's Score: _____ Rating Scale **4 3 2 1** (*See* Rubric *p. 61*)

LESSON 21: Writing a Persuasive Essay

Read a Persuasive Essay

Item   *Correct Response*
- ❏ 1.   The second sentence should be underlined.
- ❏ 2.   A star should be placed by the facts *More than 13% of all American families lived below the poverty line; It cost about 50 million dollars just to launch the rocket.* Accept other reasonable responses.
- ❏ 3.   Possible responses: *Statistics tell a troubling story . . . ; These families desperately need help . . .*
- ❏ 4.   The check mark should be by *voters.*

Write a Persuasive Essay Check whether the student has
- ❏ selected a current affairs issue as a topic.
- ❏ identified the audience to be addressed.
- ❏ used the organizer to plan the essay.
- ❏ evaluated the first draft critically, and revised it.

Evaluating the Personal Narrative Check whether the student has
- ❏ stated an opinion in the first paragraph.
- ❏ given reasons to support the opinion in the second paragraph.
- ❏ provided facts to support each reason.
- ❏ included an emotional appeal and at least one emotional word.
- ❏ restated the opinion in the final paragraph.
- ❏ given readers a call to action at the end of the essay.
- ❏ used correct capitalization, spelling, and punctuation.

Perfect Score: 15 Student's Score: _____ Rating Scale **4 3 2 1** (*See* Rubric *p. 61*)

Student's Name _____

Use check marks to indicate items answered correctly and objectives fulfilled.

LESSON 32: Writing an Explanation

Read an Explanation

Item   Correct Response
- ❑ 1. how an elevator works
- ❑ 2. The sentence beginning with these words should be underlined: *A pulley is a simple lifting device . . .*
- ❑ 3. The following sentence should be circled: *The counterweight balances the weight of the elevator.*
- ❑ 4. The X should appear by the counterweight; the star should appear by the pulley; a check mark should appear by each guard rail.
- ❑ 5. because an elevator works by using the power of the pulley

Write an Explanation Check whether the student has
- ❑ selected and researched a topic.
- ❑ used the organizer to plan information.
- ❑ evaluated the first draft and made revisions to improve it.

Evaluating the Problem/Solution Paragraph Check whether the student has
- ❑ included a topic sentence in the first paragraph.
- ❑ explained the steps of the process in sequence, where appropriate.
- ❑ sketched a diagram that clarifies the explanation.
- ❑ used language that is appropriate to the audience.
- ❑ explained unfamiliar terms.
- ❑ used complete sentences.
- ❑ capitalized and punctuated correctly.
- ❑ spelled most words correctly.

Perfect Score: 16 Student's Score: _____ Rating Scale **4 3 2 1** (*See* Rubric *p. 61*)

LESSON 43: Writing a Persuasive Essay

Read a Persuasive Essay

Item   Correct Response
- ❑ 1. The sentence beginning with these words should be underlined: *I feel that the First Amendment . . .*
- ❑ 2. The star should be by the second paragraph.
- ❑ 3. The third paragraph should be circled. **Emotional words:** *barged; outraged*
- ❑ 4. Tell the store owners how you feel and write to the record companies.

Write a Persuasive Essay Check whether the student has
- ❑ understood that the writing process is broken down into five distinct steps.
- ❑ brainstormed different topic ideas, and chosen one.
- ❑ organized facts and emotional appeals before writing.
- ❑ understood the purpose of a first draft.
- ❑ revised the first draft. (Ask the student to show you the first draft and describe what he or she did to revise it.)

Evaluating the Persuasive Paragraph Check whether the student has
- ❑ stated an opinion in the first paragraph.
- ❑ restated the opinion in the last paragraph.
- ❑ included facts that support the opinion in the second paragraph.
- ❑ included an emotional appeal and at least one emotional word.
- ❑ given readers a call to action at the end of the essay.
- ❑ used correct capitalization, spelling, and punctuation.

Perfect Score: 15 Student's Score: _____ Rating Scale **4 3 2 1** (*See* Rubric *p. 61*)

Student's Name _____

Use check marks to indicate items answered correctly and objectives fulfilled.

LESSON 54: Writing a Problem/Solution Essay

Read a Problem/Solution Essay

Item   *Correct Response*
- ❑ 1.   Because of responsibilities at home, he was arriving at work nearly 30 minutes late.
- ❑ 2.   The sentences that begin with these words should be underlined: *Because of these responsibilities . . . ; This caused problems there . . .*
- ❑ 3.   The star should be by the final paragraph.
- ❑ 4.   The sentences that begin with these words should be circled: *After school every day . . . ; Then I have to wait with him . . .*
- ❑ 5.   He seems pleased with the solution.
- ❑ 6.   The last sentence should be underlined.

Write a Problem/Solution Essay   Check whether the student has
- ❑ selected a problem from personal experience.
- ❑ identified pertinent background information.
- ❑ used the organizer to plan the essay.
- ❑ evaluated and revised the first draft.

Evaluating the Problem/Solution Essay   Check whether the student has
- ❑ described a problem in the first paragraph.
- ❑ described a solution in the following paragraphs.
- ❑ told how he or she felt about the solution in the last paragraph.
- ❑ included pertinent information, not unimportant details.
- ❑ described events in their correct sequence.
- ❑ used the first-person voice.
- ❑ used punctuation and capitalization correctly.
- ❑ spelled most words correctly.

Perfect Score: 18   Student's Score: _____   Rating Scale **4 3 2 1** (*See* Rubric *p. 61*)

LESSON 65: Writing a Résumé

Read a Résumé

Item   *Correct Response*
- ❑ 1.   two; the following sentences should be circled: *Spin Records, New York, NY; Mack's Music, Rochester, NY*
- ❑ 2.   A star should appear by the following sentences: *Reading Tutor . . . ; Basketball Coach . . .*
- ❑ 3.   yes; 1999
- ❑ 4.   The check mark should be by the part entitled *Additional Skills*.

Write a Résumé   Check whether the student has
- ❑ used the organizer to list education, experiences, and objective.
- ❑ followed the format of the sample résumé.
- ❑ evaluated, corrected, and revised the draft three times.

Evaluating the Résumé   Check whether the student has
- ❑ included his or her full name, address, and telephone number at the top of the résumé.
- ❑ included relevant information from each category in the organizer.
- ❑ included dates that indicate *when* and *how long* events occurred.
- ❑ listed the most recent experience first in each category.
- ❑ used correct capitalization and punctuation.
- ❑ spelled every word correctly.

Perfect Score: 13   Student's Score: _____   Rating Scale **4 3 2 1** (*See* Rubric *p. 61*)

Student's Name _____

Use check marks to indicate items answered correctly and objectives fulfilled.

LESSON 76: Writing a Story

Read a Story

Item Correct Response

❑ 1. A box should be drawn around the names *Marta* and *Sandra*. A circle should be drawn around the names *Sergio, Sara, Monique, Sam, Marta's mother,* and *Uncle Pete.*

❑ 2. Possible responses: **when**—*More than a week had passed; The next day* (Students might also identify details that show the story takes place in the present, such as CDs, photos, and high school.); **where**—*Uncle Pete's house; the school library*

❑ 3. Marta's house, including all her possessions, had burnt down; she was still feeling very sad. The sentences beginning with these words should be underlined: *Everything she had owned . . . ; She didn't feel like doing anything . . .* Accept other reasonable responses.

❑ 4. The sentences beginning with these words should be underlined: *Hey! Here's the deal . . . ; Her friends had helped to remind her . . .* Accept other reasonable responses.

❑ 5. An X should appear by each bit of dialogue.

Write a Story Check whether the student has

❑ brainstormed different topic ideas, and chosen one.

❑ used the story map to organize ideas.

❑ revised the story. (Review the first draft and have the student explain how it was revised.)

Evaluating the Story Check whether the student has

❑ included a beginning, a middle, and an end.

❑ introduced the characters at the beginning of the story.

❑ revealed the setting of the story.

❑ told the story in the third-person voice.

❑ made clear the sequence of events from problem to resolution.

❑ used dialogue in a way that brings the story to life.

❑ used capitalization and punctuation correctly.

❑ spelled most words correctly.

Perfect Score: 16   Student's Score: _____   Rating Scale **4 3 2 1** (*See* Rubric *p. 61*)

LESSON 87: Writing a Job Application Letter

Read a Job Application Letter

Item   Correct Response

❑ 1. *sales assistant* should be underlined; a circle should be drawn around *yesterday's newspaper*

❑ 2. An X should appear by the sentences beginning with these words: *I am a devoted music fan; I know a lot about . . . ; I am an eager . . .; I feel very comfortable . . .; I'm outgoing . . .*

❑ 3. A circle should be drawn around the words *excited; anxious; exciting environment; welcome*

❑ 4. two

❑ 5. The check mark should be by the last sentence.

Write a Job Application Letter Check whether the student has

❑ understood that the writing process is broken down into five distinct steps.

❑ used the prewriting step to plan the letter.

❑ understood the purpose of a first draft.

❑ revised the first draft to improve it.

❑ proofread the second draft.

Evaluating the Story Check whether the student has

❑ used the format of a business letter.

❑ begun by describing the job being applied for and telling how he/she learned about it.

❑ given reasons why he or she would be an excellent candidate for the job.

❑ used convincing language.

❑ described past job experience.

❑ given at least one reference.

❑ capitalized and punctuated correctly.

❑ spelled all words correctly.

Perfect Score: 18   Student's Score: _____   Rating Scale **4 3 2 1** (*See* Rubric *p. 61*)

Answer Keys for Student Lesson Pages

Lesson 1

PART I

1. .	5. F	9. F	13. F
2. F	6. .	10. .	14. .
3. F	7. F	11. F	
4. .	8. .	12. .	

PART II

Sentences may vary.

15. Settlers called these shaggy beasts buffalo.
16. Bison supplied the Plains Indians with food, shelter, and clothing.
17. The hides were made into leather for tents, clothes, and robes.
18. When settlers came west by railroad, they seldom used bison for clothing or food.
19. They usually shot them for sport.
20. The bison disappeared at an alarming rate.
21. Then laws were passed to protect them.

Lesson 2

PART I

1. (?) INT	4. (! or .) IMP	7. (?) INT	10. (.) D
2. (.) D	5. (?) INT	8. (!) E	11. (.) IMP
3. (!) E	6. (.) D	9. (?) INT	

PART II

Answers will vary.

Lesson 3

PART I

1. Native Americans; invented; game
2. Iroquois; played; it
3. lacrosse; had; name
4. Baggataway; resembled; war
5. competitors; played; game
6. organizers; placed; goals
7. competitors; played; game
8. players; play; game
9. teams; have; players
10. game; has kept; excitement
11. sticks; do resemble; equipment
12. stick; has; pocket
13. Players; catch; ball
14. opponents; might knock; ball
15. players; can throw; balls
16. players; wear; helmets

PART II

Answers will vary.

Lesson 4

PART I

1. escape; readers
2. fame, fortune; Ms. Christie
3. millions; customers
4. detectives; world
5. skills (no indirect object)
6. knowledge (no indirect object)
7. publisher (no indirect object)
8. manuscripts; editors
9. words, nothing; Ms. Christie
10. talent; world

PART II

Answers may vary.

11. "The Mysterious Affair at Styles" gave the detective story a new voice.
12. Novels, stories, and a play have given Christie's admirers much pleasure.
13. Travel to distant lands gave Christie ideas for unusual settings for stories.
14. I will give my brother an Agatha Christie novel for his birthday.

Lesson 5

PART I

1. games; are; games; predicate noun
2. reflexes; are; necessary; predicate adjective
3. Games; are; new; predicate adjective
4. Montague Redgrave; may have been; wizard; predicate noun
5. 1871; was; date; predicate noun
6. game; was; marvel; predicate noun
7. game; was; favorite; predicate noun
8. W. M. McManus; was; designer; predicate noun
9. machines; were; novelty; predicate noun
10. They; are; popular; predicate adjective
11. inventor; was; maker; predicate noun
12. Chicago; became; center; predicate noun
13. figures; were; handsome; predicate adjective
14. games; were; type; predicate noun
15. cost; was; penny; predicate noun
16. games; are; valuable; predicate adjective

PART II

Answers will vary.

Lesson 6

PART I

1. *Angela's Ashes*; is; memoir
2. Frank McCourt; describes; childhood
3. life; was; hard
4. family; was; poor
5. They; had; food
6. childhood; was; miserable
7. book; is; funny
8. McCourt; shows; humor
9. father; told; stories
10. Many; described; adventures
11. Cuchulain; is; hero
12. McCourt; inherited; talent
13. *Angela's Ashes*; won; Pulitzer Prize
14. book; has sold; copies

PART II

Answers will vary.

Lesson 7

PART I

1. Are
2. seen
3. does
4. Wasn't
5. rides, jumps
6. doesn't
7. are
8. was
9. has
10. has
11. becomes, has

PART II

~~don't~~ doesn't; ~~have~~ has; ~~seen~~ has seen; ~~Aren't~~ Isn't; ~~ain't~~ isn't; ~~has~~ have; ~~Do~~ Does; ~~ain't~~ am not; ~~has~~ have

Synonym Watch: audacity—daring

Lesson 8

PART I

1. <u>daniel</u>, <u>hale</u>, <u>williams</u>, <u>hollidaysburg</u>, <u>pennsylvania</u>
2. <u>left</u>
3. <u>then</u>, <u>chicago</u>, <u>illinois</u>, <u>chicago</u>, <u>medical</u>, <u>college</u>
4. <u>daniel</u>, <u>williams</u>, <u>june</u>
5. <u>several</u>, <u>provident</u>, <u>hospital</u>, <u>chicago</u>
6. <u>one</u>
7. <u>with</u>, <u>dr.</u>, <u>williams</u>
8. <u>the</u>, <u>african</u>, <u>american</u>
9. <u>freedman's</u>, <u>hospital</u>, <u>washington</u>, <u>d. c.</u>, <u>united</u>, <u>states</u>
10. <u>dr.</u>, <u>williams</u>

PART II

11. Doctors from Johns Hopkins University and the University of Pennsylvania used to visit to watch Dr. Williams operate.
12. Once he traveled to Tuskegee Institute in Alabama to operate on Booker T. Washington's personal secretary.
13. Dr. Williams left Washington, D.C., and returned to Provident Hospital after President Grover Cleveland left office.
14. In February 1898 he married Alice Johnson, daughter of the sculptor Moses Jacob Ezekiel.
15. Paul L. Dunbar, a famous African American poet, wrote a poem for the occasion.

Lesson 9

1. "Tombstone, Arizona, was one of the wildest towns in the old West," said Clara.
2. "Clara, who was Ed Schieffelin?" asked Bert.
3. "Wasn't he a slow, careful, persistent prospector?" he continued.
4. Clara answered, "Yes, Schieffelin had searched in Oregon, California, and Nevada with little success."
5. "Then he began searching the hills near the San Pedro River in southern Arizona," she said.
6. "What a hot, dry, empty area that is!" said Tamika.
7. "Schieffelin searched for a long time without having any luck," Clara said.
8. "Rattlesnakes, Gila monsters, and bandits lurked in the rocky canyons," she continued.
9. Then Clara said, "Schieffelin told a soldier that he would find something useful out there."
10. "What was the soldier's reply?" asked Tamika.

11. "The soldier told Schieffelin that the only useful thing he would find was his own tombstone," said Clara.
12. "Schieffelin, however, found a rich, wide, and promising vein of silver," she explained.
13. "He named this claim the Tombstone," Clara continued.
14. "So the name of the claim was an answer to the soldier's cruel reply!" exclaimed Tamika.
15. "Yes," said Clara, "and soon the town of Tombstone, Arizona, was born."
16. "Toughnut Street, Allen Street, Fremont Street, and Safford Street were laid out," she explained.
17. "Do you know what happened on Thursday, October 27, 1881, at the O.K. Corral?" Clara asked Tamika.
18. "Didn't Wyatt Earp, his brothers, and Doc Holliday duel Ike Clanton's cowboys?" asked Bert.
19. "You're right," said Tamika.
20. "I know that Tombstone's slogan is 'the town too tough to die,'" said Bert.

Word Whiz: conclusive; reclusive; inclusive

Lesson 11

PART I

1. F
2. F
3. .
4. .
5. F
6. .

PART II

7. (!) E
8. (.) D
9. (.) IMP
10. (?) INT

PART III

11. (giggles); me
12. (dogs) (no indirect object)
13. (fame); dogs

PART IV

14. <u>photos</u>; <u>are</u>; (funny); predicate adjective
15. <u>dogs</u>; <u>look</u>; (dignified); predicate adjective
16. <u>William Wegman</u>; <u>is</u>; (photographer); predicate noun

Lesson 12

PART I

1. simple
2. simple
3. <u>Resort cities line the bay</u>, (and) <u>Vesuvius rises in the background</u>. compound
4. <u>On sunny days there is blue sky and blue water</u>, (and) <u>the mountain stands between them</u>. compound
5. simple
6. <u>The Roman city of Pompeii was located there</u>, (but) <u>it disappeared in a single day</u>. compound
7. <u>Vesuvius is an active volcano</u>, (and) <u>it erupts from time to time</u>. compound
8. simple
9. simple
10. <u>People could have left temporarily</u>, (or) <u>they could have abandoned the city entirely</u>. compound
11. simple
12. simple
13. <u>Smoke darkened the sky</u>, (and) <u>ash and stones rained on Pompeii</u>. compound
14. simple
15. <u>The sun came out two days later</u>, (but) <u>Pompeii was gone</u>. compound

PART II Answers will vary.

Lesson 13

PART I

Answers may vary.

1. A young man had hiked up a canyon trail, but he could not climb back down.
2. A loose rock had caused him to fall, and he had broken his ankle.
3. Hikers heard his cries for help, and a rescue team rushed to the scene.
4. The canyon wall was steep and treacherous, but it was the only route to the injured man.
5. The team members were expert climbers, and the victim was soon in their sight.
6. Getting the man to safety would be difficult, but the team felt confident.
7. They might carry him down themselves, or a helicopter might have to lift him out of the canyon.
8. The rescuers reached the canyon floor with the victim, and an ambulance sped him to a hospital.

PART II Answers will vary.

Lesson 14

PART I

Sentences may vary.

1. The Chinese monk I-Hsing designed and built the first mechanical clock in A.D. 725.
2. The clock was huge and very complex.
3. Other Chinese inventions are gunpowder, paper money, and the compass.
4. Thomas Edison patented the electric light and the phonograph.
5. Orville Wright and his brother Wilbur built the first successful airplane.
6. In 1826 Joseph Niépce exposed a chemical-treated metal plate to light and created the first photograph.
7. Garrett A. Morgan invented the gas mask and traffic lights.
8. Lady Ava Lovelace and Rear Admiral Grace Murray Hopper were pioneers of computer programming.

PART II

Answers may vary.

compound subject 5, 8	compound predicate noun 3
compound predicate 1, 6	compound predicate adjective 2
compound direct object 4, 7	

Lesson 15

Answers may vary.

1. Arteries carry blood through the body, and veins also carry blood. Arteries and veins carry blood through the body.
2. The heart beats in rhythm; it pumps blood constantly. The heart beats in rhythm and pumps blood constantly.
3. It receives blood from the veins, and it pumps blood into the lungs. It receives blood from the veins and pumps blood into the lungs.

4. It receives oxygenated blood from the lungs, and it pumps this blood into the arteries. It receives oxygenated blood from the lungs and pumps this blood into the arteries.
5. Blood carries oxygen to all parts of the body, and it carries nutrients to all parts of the body. Blood carries oxygen and nutrients to all parts of the body.
6. We need oxygen-rich blood constantly, and we depend on the heart to distribute it. We need oxygen-rich blood constantly and depend on the heart to distribute it.
7. The heart, blood, and lungs never rest, but they work less during sleep. The heart, blood, and lungs never rest but work less during sleep.

Lesson 16

PART I

1. Dr.	4. St.	7. Gov.	10. Sat.
2. Fri.	5. Wed.	8. Nov.	
3. Oct.	6. Rev.	9. Blvd.	

PART I

11. Is the Fahrenheit scale the best way of indicating temperature, or should we change to a different scale?
12. Water freezes at 32° Fahrenheit, and it boils at 212°F.
13. Great Britain, the United States, and other predominantly English-speaking countries commonly use this scale.
14. Most of the rest of the world uses the Celsius scale, however.
15. This scale, also called the centigrade scale, is easy to use.
16. On this scale, water freezes at 0°C, and it boils at 100°C.
17. Don't these two reference points make comparisons of temperatures easier to understand?
18. The Celsius scale is commonly used in science, engineering, and many other fields.
19. Old habits, of course, are hard to change.
20. Most people in the United States still use the Fahrenheit scale to describe the weather.
21. For instance, imagine it is August 1, a hot, muggy day.
22. Would you describe the temperature as 95°F, or would you describe it as 35°C?

Odd Word Out: The word *chisel* does not belong. The other four words could fit in the category "theater" or "drama." *Chisel* could fit in the catetgory "sculpture" or "carpentry."

Lesson 17

PART I

1.	Will's tennis shoes	6.	the bakeries' breads
2.	the children's friend	7.	the magician's trick
3.	the fans' shouts	8.	the park's carousel
4.	Emily's pen	9.	the clerk's excuses
5.	the elders' stories	10.	the women's smocks

PART II

11.	brothers'	17.	friends'
12.	mother's	18.	Katie's
13.	class's	19.	bus's
14.	bus's	20.	girls'
15.	buses'	21.	area's
16.	Diana's	22.	students'

Lesson 18

PART I

1. flies
2. valleys
3. women
4. potatoes
5. crashes
6. deer
7. pianos
8. matches
9. stories
10. mice

PART II

Sentences will vary. The plural nouns should be spelled as shown above.

PART III

15. JoAnne's
16. judges'
17. engine's
18. pattern's
19. brothers'
20. Max's

PART IV

Sentences will vary. The possessive forms should be spelled as shown above.
Near Misses: Most of the drama students seem to belong to the same clique.

Lesson 19

1. <u>desert</u>, subject; <u>place</u>, predicate noun
2. <u>land</u>, predicate noun
3. <u>rattlesnake</u>, subject; <u>creature</u>, predicate noun
4. <u>rattle</u>, subject; <u>creatures</u>, indirect object; <u>feeling</u>, direct object
5. <u>sunlight</u>, subject; <u>rocks</u>, indirect object; <u>glow</u>, direct object
6. <u>heat</u>, subject
7. <u>Sunset</u>, subject; <u>traveler</u>, indirect object; <u>relief</u>, direct object
8. <u>Nightfall</u>, subject; <u>landscape</u>, direct object
9. <u>moon</u>, subject; <u>shadows</u>, direct object
10. <u>temperatures</u>, subject; <u>occurrence</u>, predicate noun
11. <u>sky</u>, subject; <u>sight</u>, predicate noun

Lesson 20

The Battle of New Orleans

Soon after the United States won its freedom from Great Britain, the two nations were at war again. The fighting lasted more than two years, and the struggle became known as the War of 1812. The British, the Canadians, and their Native American allies won most of the land battles. On the sea, fortunately, the Americans won some victories. On January 8, 1815, a major battle was fought at New Orleans, Louisiana. British troops led by General Sir Edward Paken-ham attacked less numerous American forces led by General Andrew Jackson, known as "Old Hickory." The British attacked in closed ranks while the Americans stayed hidden. Jackson's strategy was successful. The British suffered about 2,000 casualties, but only 14 Americans died. Ironically, this battle took place several weeks after leaders of the two nations had agreed to end the war.
Synonym Watch: embarrass—humiliate

Lesson 22

PART I

1. classes
2. pastries
3. torches
4. women

PART II

5. country's
6. pitchers'
7. men's
8. friends'

PART III

9. simple
10. compound; but
11. compound; and

PART IV

Answers will vary.
12. The players and the coach celebrated their victory with shouts and cheers.
13. Most fans stayed in the stands for a long time, but some left right after the finish.
14. The star player waved to the crowd and then left the arena.

PART V

15. The anchovy, a small fish, has a salty taste.
16. Other fish, however, do not taste at all salty.
17. Do you like salty fish, or do you prefer those that aren't salty?

Lesson 23

PART I

1. <u>Jim</u>; <u>book</u>; <u>week</u>
2. <u>Greg</u>; <u>Anne</u>; <u>Jim</u>; <u>books</u>; <u>time</u>
3. <u>Jim</u>; <u>book</u>; <u>purpose</u>
4. <u>name</u>; <u>book</u>; *<u>Your Memory</u>*
5. <u>Brent</u>; <u>lunchbox</u>; <u>Jim</u>; <u>stairs</u>
6. <u>Brent</u>; <u>sandwiches</u>; <u>lunchbox</u>; <u>Jim</u>
7. <u>Jim</u>; <u>Lorre</u>; <u>concert</u>
8. <u>Jim</u>; <u>Lorre</u>; <u>house</u>; <u>taxi</u>
9. <u>librarians</u>; <u>Jim</u>; <u>dollars</u>; <u>book</u>
10. <u>expense</u>; <u>memory</u>

PART II

11. <u>He</u>, <u>it</u>; Jim, book
12. <u>They</u>, <u>he</u>, <u>them</u>; Greg, Anne, Jim, books
13. <u>he</u>, <u>it</u>; Jim, book
14. <u>it</u>; book
15. <u>He</u>, <u>it</u>; Brent, lunchbox
16. <u>He</u>, <u>them</u>, <u>he</u>, <u>it</u>, <u>him</u>; Brent, sandwiches, lunchbox (*or* Jim's lunchbox), Jim (Note that the pronoun *it* was already a pronoun in the original sentence.)
17. <u>he</u>, <u>her</u>; Jim, Lorre
18. <u>He</u>, <u>she</u>; Jim, Lorre
19. <u>They</u>, <u>him</u>, <u>it</u>; librarians, Jim, book
20. <u>it</u>, <u>his</u>; expense (Note that the pronoun *his* was already a pronoun in the original sentence.)

Lesson 24

1. subject
2. direct object
3. subject
4. object of a preposition
5. subject
6. object of a preposition
7. indirect object
8. direct object
9. subject
10. direct object
11. direct object
12. indirect object
13. subject
14. object of a preposition
15. subject
16. object of a preposition
17. subject
18. direct object
19. object of a preposition
20. indirect object

Lesson 25

PART I

1. I
2. him, me
3. I
4. me
5. us
6. she
7. we
8. he
9. They, us
10. I
11. us
12. us
13. I
14. us
15. me

PART II

16. I—subject
17. him—direct object
18. me—direct object
19. I—predicate pronoun
20. me—direct object
21. us—object of a preposition
22. she—predicate pronoun
23. we—subject
24. he—subject
25. They—subject
26. us—indirect object
27. I—subject
28. us—direct object
29. us—object of a preposition
30. I—subject
31. us—direct object
32. me—object of a preposition

Lesson 26

PART I

1. I
2. He, I
3. him, me
4. me
5. She, him
6. she, we
7. me
8. He
9. I
10. she
11. me
12. she
13. she
14. me
15. her

PART II

Answers will vary.

Lesson 27

PART I

1. your
2. their
3. his
4. her
5. Their
6. our
7. my
8. our
9. my
10. its
11. her
12. your

PART II

13. There's
14. Its
15. there's
16. it's
17. It's
18. theirs

Optional Exercise: Sentences will vary.

Lesson 28

PART I

1. their; nurses
2. she; doctor
3. his, her; doctor
4. their; Art, Marie
5. her; Greta
6. their; nurses
7. her; Dr. Adams
8. their; doctors
9. he, she; doctor
10. their; doctors

PART II

11. his
12. his
13. her
14. his, her
15. their
16. their
17. their
18. his
19. his
20. his

Lesson 29

Answers will vary.

Simon bought a used car last week. He asked Neville and Anne to help him fix it up. He and she agreed right away. They know a lot about cars, and they enjoy putting their skills to use. Neville changed the oil and the transmission fluid. He also replaced the battery. Anne told him that she admired his skill. Anne worked on the body of the car. She pounded out some dents. She also called a salvage yard and located a matching set of hubcaps. Simon borrowed a buffing machine from his brother and gave the car an expert wax job. When Simon, Neville, and Anne were done, they admired the car. Simon thanked Neville and Anne for the excellent job they had done.

Lesson 30

1. interrogative; demonstrative
2. possessive
3. possessive
4. possessive; personal; personal
5. interrogative; personal
6. indefinite; personal
7. personal; personal; demonstrative
8. personal; personal
9. compound personal; personal
10. interrogative
11. personal; compound personal
12. compound personal; demonstrative; indefinite

Lesson 31

1. Simón Bolívar, a South American general, was born in Caracas, Venezuela, on July 24, 1783.
2. He first led a group of patriots who helped win the city of Caracas from Spain.
3. Bolívar was later forced to flee to Colombia, Jamaica, and Haiti to gather an army.
4. Bolívar's victories in South America brought about the end of Spanish rule.
5. The country of Mexico has also had a stormy history of war with Spain.
6. The explorer Hernando Cortés was sent to explore Mexico in 1518.
7. Cortés had been told tales of the gold and jewels of the Aztecs.
8. The Aztec people had built Tenochtitlán, a great city on the shores of Lake Texcoco.
9. This Aztec city reminded Cortés of the Italian city of Venice.
10. Cortés and his forces laid siege to the city in May of 1521.
11. Cuautémoc, the last Aztec emperor, was forced to surrender the city to the Spaniards in August of 1521.
12. War between France and Spain in the early nineteenth century helped the cause of Mexican independence.
13. Mexico became a republic on October 4, 1824.
14. Today Mexico City is one of the largest, busiest, and most colorful cities in the world.

Lesson 33

PART I

1. he; Jim
2. their; Andy, Carla
3. she; Vera

PART II

4. I
5. me
6. them, us

7. my   8. their   9. our

10. interrogative; personal
11. personal; compound personal
12. personal, possessive

13. direct object   15. subject
14. object of a preposition

Lesson 34

The word after each underlined word should be written
   on the line.
1. This, leader; brilliant, leader; effective, container
2. large, sum; first, prize; special, contest
3. new, method; fresh, foods
4. Every, inventor; clever, inventor; French, inventor;
   that, prize; big, prize
5. many, years; this, problem; difficult, problem
6. fresh, foods; sturdy, bottles
7. warm, bottles; steamy, bottles; dense, cork
8. full, bottles; large, pot; hot, water
9. This, method; simple, method; effective, method;
   destructive, bacteria
10. This, Parisian; bright, Parisian; patient, Parisian;
   rich, prize

Lesson 35

1. numerous; reptiles
2. smaller; numbers
3. present; tortoises
4. isolated; Galapagos Islands
5. difficult; survival
6. aware; sailors
7. weary, bored, hungry; sailors
8. ideal; stop
9. delicious; meat
10. easy; Capture
11. scarce; Tortoises
12. long, sad; story
13. extinct; types
14. uncertain; future
Word Whiz: conserve, console, consume

Lesson 36

1. most important
2. oldest
3. smaller
4. biggest
5. better
6. more resistant
7. sweeter
8. best

9. most primitive
10. oldest
11. harder
12. best
13. earliest
14. starchiest or most starchy
15. more popular
16. taller
17. most productive
Name That Job: farmer. Check students' paragraphs for
accuracy.

Lesson 37

1. attempted, boldly
2. gathered, eagerly
3. would begin, there
4. rose, shakily
5. was cheering, Soon, wildly
6. was, certainly
7. was, lost, temporarily
8. went, suddenly
9. began dripping, Then, horribly
10. piloted, skillfully
11. landed, smoothly
12. had, achieved, courageously
13. pursued, tirelessly
14. lost, inexplicably
15. perished, apparently, tragically
16. have, been found, ever

Answers will vary.

Lesson 38

1. incredibly; beautiful; adj.
2. almost; vertical; adj.
3. quite; meticulously; adv.
4. painstakingly; slow; adj.
5. slightly; curved; adj.
6. infinitesimally; higher; adv.
7. rather; confident; adj.
8. very; foolishly; adv.
9. dangerously; fast; adv.
10. just; barely; adv.
11. extremely; grateful; adj.
12. Very; gingerly; adv.

Sentences will vary.

Lesson 39

1. faster
2. more swiftly
3. fastest
4. slower
5. Most often
6. more swiftly
7. more often
8. more effectively
9. worst
10. more likely

11. slower or more slowly
12. better
13. more often
14. slowest or most slowly
15. worse
16. more skillfully
17. longer
18. better

Lesson 40

PART I

1. <u>At</u> the age; <u>of</u> ten; <u>in</u> cars
2. <u>on</u> blocks; <u>in</u> the backyard
3. <u>on</u> it
4. <u>at</u> seven; <u>in</u> the morning; <u>with</u> the carburetor
5. <u>By</u> my sixteenth birthday; <u>from</u> a dozen cars
6. <u>in</u> a garage; <u>on</u> weekends; <u>during</u> the summer
7. <u>in</u> six months; <u>with</u> serious mechanical problems
8. <u>at</u> the end; <u>of</u> a year; <u>of</u> hard work
9. <u>from</u> my backyard; <u>to</u> a local racetrack
10. <u>in</u> the quarter-mile; <u>from</u> my ride
11. <u>with</u> luck; <u>at</u> Bonneville

PART II

Sentences will vary.
Antonym Watch: bona fide—counterfeit

Lesson 41

PART I

1. of the detective; hair
2. for this odd disguise; reason
3. of the Silver Scream Waxworks; owner
4. of his wax figures; faces
5. of the detective; task
6. of this mad torcher; capture
7. in the building; guard
8. beside a wax Humphrey Bogart; pedestal

PART II

9. above the wax Elizabeth I; appeared
10. down the aisle; was creeping
11. toward the detective's face; raised
12. From the pedestal; leaped
13. with an iron grip; grabbed
14. by the torcher's face; was shocked
15. To her surprise; had caught
16. in her life; had had

Connecting Meanings: preclude—make impossible; proceed—continue; precede—come before. Check students' sentences to be sure they use *preclude*, *proceed*, and *precede* correctly.

Lesson 42

Woody's Land

In the southwestern town of Okemah, Oklahoma, Woody Guthrie was born in 1912. He was a poor boy with itchy feet and great talents. During his youth he rode freight trains all over the United States. His uncle had taught him to play the guitar, and his guitar was always with him. He composed songs about penniless travelers, about hard-luck farmers, and even about the Bonneville Dam. He traveled the country from New York to California. He wrote a book about himself, too, called <u>Bound for Glory</u>. He was just becoming famous when he became very ill. He spent the last fifteen years of his life in a hospital. However, many thousands of people still sing his songs today. Hasn't everyone heard his song "This Land Is Your Land"? The Okemah Library has paid him a tribute. His music was recorded for the Library of

Congress. A power plant in the Pacific Northwest was named in his honor. His son, Arlo, also a fine folksinger, helps keep his father's legacy alive. Woody Guthrie will long be remembered by the country he loved.

Lesson 44

PARTS I–V

Answers will vary.

Lesson 45

PART I

1. <u>live</u>; action
2. <u>become</u>; linking
3. <u>are</u>; linking
4. <u>do catch</u>; action
5. <u>hunt</u>; action
6. <u>have</u>; action
7. <u>use</u>; action
8. <u>is</u>; linking
9. <u>makes</u>; action
10. <u>tell</u>; action
11. <u>are</u>; linking
12. <u>have</u>; action
13. <u>is</u>; linking
14. <u>is</u>; linking

PART II

Sentences will vary.
Connecting Meanings: conscience—sense of right and wrong; conscious—aware; consent—agree to. Check students' sentences to be sure they use *conscience*, *conscious*, and *consent* correctly.

Lesson 46

PART I

1. goes
2. reads
3. are, keeps
4. Do, speaks
5. has
6. meets, goes
7. make
8. is
9. was
10. gets
11. last
12. likes
13. speaks
14. shops
15. see
16. tries
17. agree, is
18. wants

PART II

Sentences will vary. Check for proper subject-verb agreement.

Lesson 47

PART I

1. is
2. speaks
3. listens
4. tell
5. gives
6. reflects
7. reveal
8. was
9. knows
10. think
11. is
12. find
13. have
14. stare
15. grasps

PART II

Sentences will vary. Check for proper subject-verb agreement.
Word Whiz: exclaim, exclude, exchange

Lesson 48

PART I

1. <u>teaches</u>; present
2. <u>will teach</u>; future
3. <u>adds</u>; present
4. <u>bought</u>; past
5. <u>had</u>; past
6. <u>taught</u>; past
7. <u>gave</u>; past
8. <u>want</u>; present
9. <u>makes</u>; present
10. <u>uses</u>; present
11. <u>was</u>; past
12. <u>left</u>; past
13. <u>imported</u>; past
14. <u>Will travel</u>; future

Sentences will vary. The past forms of the verbs are shown.
15. did   16. drew   17. drank   18. went
Connecting Meanings: facial—having to do with the face; facile—easy; façade—front (of a building). Check students' sentences to be sure they use *facial, facile,* and *façade* correctly.

Lesson 49

PART I

1. <u>have grown</u>; present perfect
2. <u>had become</u>; past perfect
3. <u>had been called</u>; past perfect
4. <u>have remained</u>; present perfect
5. <u>had learned</u>; past perfect
6. <u>had tasted</u>; past perfect
7. <u>had eaten</u>; past perfect
8. <u>will have eaten</u>; future perfect
9. <u>have been grown</u>; present perfect
10. <u>have changed</u>; present perfect
11. <u>had used</u>; past perfect
12. <u>had discovered</u>; past perfect
13. <u>have become</u>; present perfect
14. <u>have recommended</u>; present perfect
15. <u>will have created</u>; future perfect
16. <u>will have developed</u>; future perfect

PART II

Sentences will vary. The tense forms of the verbs are shown.
17. will have tried   18. had gone

Lesson 50

PART I

1. <u>was found</u>; passive
2. <u>found</u>; active
3. <u>robbed</u>; active
4. <u>was robbed</u>; passive
5. <u>reported</u>; active
6. <u>was reported</u>; passive
7. <u>were spent</u>; passive
8. <u>spent</u>; active
9. <u>was captured</u>; passive
10. <u>captured</u>; active
11. <u>were ended</u>; passive
12. <u>ended</u>; active

PART II

Sentences will vary.
13. Professor A. L. Kroeber gave Ishi a home at the University of California.
14. In his new situation, Ishi showed wisdom and dignity.
15. Theodora Kroeber, wife of A. L. Kroeber, wrote a biography entitled <u>Ishi: Last of His Tribe</u>.

Lesson 51

PART I

1. there's
2. it's
3. won't
4. doesn't
5. haven't
6. they're
7. you're
8. we've
9. who's
10. hasn't

PART II

Answers will vary.
11. won't *or* shouldn't
12. didn't *or* wouldn't
13. isn't
14. aren't
15. I've *or* We've
16. Who's
17. you're
18. She's

PART III

Sentences will vary.

Lesson 52

PART I

1. is
2. appears
3. prints
4. comes *or* came
5. issued
6. had
7. voted
8. called
9. is
10. issued
11. guaranteed
12. coined
13. supervises
14. are
15. wears
16. last

PART II

Sentences will vary.

Lesson 53

PART I

1. <u>j</u>amaica is one of the islands in the <u>c</u>aribbean <u>s</u>ea.
2. <u>k</u>ingston, <u>j</u>amaica, has almost the same temperature summer and winter.
3. <u>t</u>he <u>b</u>lue <u>m</u>ountains rise in the eastern part of the island, and heavy rains fall there.
4. <u>t</u>he hurricane season, <u>a</u>ugust to <u>n</u>ovember, brings damaging storms.
5. <u>c</u>hristopher <u>c</u>olumbus landed on <u>j</u>amaica in 1494, and for a brief time he held title to it.
6. <u>t</u>he <u>a</u>rawak people had lived there for centuries, but the <u>s</u>panish invaders killed most of them.
7. <u>t</u>he <u>s</u>panish brought in enslaved <u>a</u>fricans to work on plantations.
8. <u>t</u>he island became a <u>b</u>ritish colony in 1670.
9. <u>p</u>eople from <u>e</u>ngland, <u>s</u>cotland, <u>c</u>hina, <u>i</u>ndia, and the <u>m</u>iddle <u>e</u>ast came to settle in <u>j</u>amaica in the eighteenth, nineteenth, and twentieth centuries.
10. <u>o</u>n <u>a</u>ugust 6, 1962, <u>j</u>amaica gained its independence.
11. <u>a</u> <u>j</u>amaican musician, <u>b</u>ob <u>m</u>arley, became famous around the world in the 1970s.
12. <u>r</u>eggae, the music he played, has its roots in <u>j</u>amaican folk and popular music.
13. <u>i</u>t also contains elements of <u>a</u>frican traditional music, calypso music, and <u>n</u>orth <u>a</u>merican pop music.
14. <u>j</u>amaica lost a great artist when <u>m</u>arley died of cancer in <u>m</u>iami, <u>f</u>lorida, in 1981.
15. <u>r</u>ita <u>m</u>arley, <u>b</u>ob <u>m</u>arley's wife, has had a long career as a singer in reggae groups.
16. <u>z</u>iggy <u>m</u>arley, <u>b</u>ob and <u>r</u>ita's son, began a successful musical career in 1988 with the release of the album *conscious party*.

PART II

Sentences will vary.

Lesson 55

PART I

Sentences will vary.

PART II

Sentences will vary.

5. rode   6. saw   7. knew

PART III

Sentences will vary.

8. (has *or* have) ridden   10. (has *or* have) known
9. (has *or* have) seen

PART IV

Sentences will vary.

11. they're   12. won't

PART V

13. past   15. present perfect
14. past perfect   16. future

Lesson 56

PART I

1. borrowed, car
2. fallen, tree
3. rented, truck
4. dented, fender
5. unplanned, delay
6. prepared, dinner
7. torn, curtains
8. brewed, coffee
9. rolling, hills
10. Congested, traffic

PART II

11. sitting on the table, radio
12. taken from other radios, parts
13. borrowed from her friend, tools
14. soldered together, Wires
15. bought at a hardware store, plans
16. ordered from the East Coast, Parts
17. broadcast from Canada, programs
18. repairing computers, job
19. hiring trainees for computer maintenance positions, person
20. requiring math skills and technical knowledge, Jobs

Lesson 57

PART I

Answers may vary.

1. Standing at the bus stop, Tony and his boss witnessed the accident.
2. Taking the turn too fast, the truck ran into a parked car.
3. Hitting the car hard, the truck caused serious damage.
4. Arriving at the scene moments later, police officers took Tony's statement.

PART II

Answers may vary.

5. Walking to the store, I saw a new restaurant.
6. Jane gave a book written by Thomas Sanchez to her niece.

7. Humming a lively tune, Carmen walked past a statue.
8. I gave my sister a roast turkey wrapped in aluminum foil.

Lesson 58

PART I

1. Tumbling; subject
2. packing; direct object
3. Waiting; subject
4. Worrying; subject
5. discussing; direct object
6. Snorkeling; subject
7. snapping; predicate noun
8. teaching; predicate noun

PART II

Sentences will vary.

Lesson 59

PART I

1. Calling sumo a Japanese version of boxing
2. striking an opponent with a closed fist
3. Tripping an opponent
4. playing basketball for his school team
5. learning this ancient Japanese sport
6. Attending sumo training camp in Tokyo
7. winning bout after bout
8. Becoming the first non-Japanese grand champion of sumo in 1993

PART II

Sentences will vary.

Lesson 60

PART I

1. to find   2. To locate   3. to recover   4. To find

PART II

5. to search   7. to fight
6. to be found   8. to prove

PART III

9. to know   11. to yell
10. to outrun   12. to fall

Antonym Watch: spare—lavish

Lesson 61

PART I

1. to show a video replay of the match
2. to swim
3. to ask the tennis pro some questions
4. to play a drop shot
5. to practice more
6. To win a tournament
7. to bring their trophies

PART II

Sentences will vary.

Lesson 62

PART I

1. wide
2. empty
3. wound
4. watchful
5. slim
6. keep
7. warning
8. rules
9. bones
10. under

PART II

11. sharp
12. close
13. quiet
14. worst
15. superior
16. morose
17. lower
18. smooth
19. penalty
20. worthless

Lesson 63

PART I

1. carry
2. tell
3. looks
4. supply
5. think
6. provides
7. claim
8. recommends
9. sell
10. is

PART II

Sentences will vary.

Lesson 64

PART I

1. run-on
2. comma splice
3. fragment
4. run-on
5. comma splice
6. fragment
7. run-on
8. fragment

PART II

Answers may vary.
9. Many astronauts get space sick, but some do not.
10. NASA scientists wanted to find the reason, so they conducted an experiment.
11. They put tanks of fish in orbit on the space shuttle.
12. Many experienced space sickness, and they swam in circles.
13. Others didn't get sick, and neither did their descendants.
14. What was the cause of the difference between the two groups of fish?
15. Some had better eyesight, and they were the healthy ones in space.
16. Is there a connection between good eyesight and resistance to space sickness?

Lesson 66

PART I

1. (stubbed)   2. (setting)   3. (growing) in the window

PART II

4. (Saving) short pieces of string
5. (waiting) for a bus
6. (knitting) a muffler

PART III

7. (to stay) for dinner
8. (to break) old habits
9. (To become) a trapeze artist
10. (to leave)

PART IV

11. carries   12. stay   13. leads   14. belongs

Lesson 67

1. The ocean's beauty attracts us (whenever) we look out to sea.
2. The ocean scares us, too, (because) we are not at home there.
3. (Although) we travel on and under the surface, the ocean is not our home.
4. The ocean is a place (where) strange and sometimes deadly creatures live.
5. (Although) we have learned a great deal, much remains a mystery.
6. (Since) the first time we humans went to sea, the shark has frightened us.
7. Sharks are feared and hated (because) some are fierce killers.
8. (When) we see a fin above the water, we feel a stab of fear.
9. No one enters the water (if) a shark is swimming nearby.
10. (If) we understood sharks better, we might not be so afraid.
11. (Though) all sharks are carnivorous, most species of sharks are not dangerous to people.
12. (Although) the whale shark is huge, it is usually harmless.
13. Many other sharks will not attack (unless) they are aroused.
14. A shark often turns away (if) it meets a healthy creature its own size.
15. (While) a shark looks big to us, we also look big to the shark.
16. Some species of sharks deserve their reputations as killers, (since) they often attack people.
17. (If) we consider size and viciousness, the great white is the most dangerous shark.
18. (Although) most sharks live in salt water, one dangerous shark lives in fresh water in Lake Nicaragua.

Antonym Watch: prey, predator

Lesson 68

PART I

1. Sheila Young, won; she, became; CX
2. she, won; Young, had won; CX
3. Young, had won
4. speed skaters, bicyclists, compete
5. They, can do; they, use; CX
6. Sue Novara, might have duplicated; she, had skated; CX
7. Novara, won, competed
8. Novara, broke; she, was considered; CX

PART II

Sentences will vary.

Lesson 69
Answers may vary.
1. Although the ship was supposedly unsinkable, it sank quickly.
2. There was much excitement when the *Titanic* sailed from England.
3. Since this was the ship's first voyage, many famous people were aboard.
4. The ship was traveling fast because the captain hoped for a speed record.
5. While the passengers were having fun, the ship rammed an iceberg.
6. If the night was clear, why did no one see the iceberg in time?
7. Everyone was ordered on deck as the ship began to sink.
8. Although there were nearly 2,300 people aboard, the lifeboats had room for only 950.
9. Another ship rescued 700 people after the *Titanic* sank.

Lesson 70

PART I

1. people who want better vocabularies
2. Latin, which was the language of ancient Rome
3. Territory, which means "an area of land"
4. word that means "land" or "earth"
5. person who can recognize this root
6. words that come from the same root
7. language that citizens of ancient Athens spoke
8. age when people are exploring space
9. person whose job is the exploration of space
10. terms that mean "star" and "sailor"

PART II

11. which
12. that (*or* which)
13. which
14. who
15. that (*or* which)
16. that (*or* which)
17. who
18. that (*or* which)
19. that (*or* which)
20. who

Lesson 71
1. Although I had visited South America several times,
2. that I felt very refreshed from it
3. After our plane landed in Mexico City,
4. When we finished unpacking,
5. because the city is at a high altitude
6. Since Mexico City has many fine restaurants,
7. that I'm still discussing its sights
8. After we drove through the city one last time,
9. As we drove,
10. when we saw Popocatepetl, the famous peak
11. Although it was close,
12. that we could see the peak clearly
13. until we reached the Taxco turnoff
14. Because we were tired after a busy week in Mexico City,
15. where we could relax on the beach
16. When you spend a week in Acapulco,
Name That Job: This person probably sews clothing for a living. Check students' paragraphs for accuracy.

Lesson 72
Answers will vary.
1. Anne studied literature at a state college, and she worked for a publisher.
   After Anne studied literature at a state college, she worked for a publisher.
2. She was still in school, but two of her stories were published.
   While she was still in school, two of her stories were published.
3. Anne graduated from college, and she wrote for magazines.
   When Anne graduated from college, she wrote for magazines.
4. Her first story was rejected, but she sold many stories over time.
   Although her first story was rejected, she sold many stories over time.
5. She did a great deal of research, and her stories were interesting.
   Because she did a great deal of research, her stories were interesting.
6. Anne wrote a very fine story, and she expanded it into a novel.
   After Anne wrote a very fine story, she expanded it into a novel.

Lesson 73

PART I

1. ~~and stuff like that~~
2. ~~it~~
3. ~~he~~
4. ~~it,~~ ~~like~~
5. ~~went~~ ~~and~~
6. ~~go and,~~ ~~or something~~
7. ~~and things,~~ ~~of~~
8. ~~at~~
9. ~~there~~
10. ~~he,~~ ~~gone and~~
11. ~~it,~~ ~~over~~ *or* ~~above~~
12. ~~of,~~ ~~there~~
13. ~~he,~~ ~~up~~
14. ~~they,~~ *or* ~~anything~~
15. ~~here~~
16. ~~it,~~ ~~like~~

PART II

Answers may vary.
17. Jack London worked at Alaskan mining camps himself.
18. Where are you going with that book?
19. I'll lend you this library card so you can get your own copy.

Lesson 74
1. ~~won~~ one; ~~grate~~ great
2. ~~head~~ headed; ~~four~~ for
3. ~~play~~ played; ~~their~~ there
4. ~~were~~ was; ~~knew~~ new
5. ~~a~~ an; ~~beet~~ beat
6. ~~urge~~ urged; ~~formerly~~ formally
7. ~~become~~ became; ~~right~~ write
8. ~~witch~~ which; ~~soled~~ sold
9. ~~become~~ became; ~~real~~ very
10. ~~was~~ were; ~~them~~ those
11. ~~wood~~ would; ~~two~~ to
12. ~~continue~~ continued; ~~we're~~ were
13. ~~were~~ was; ~~spend~~ spent

14. ~~an~~ a; ~~broked~~ broke
15. ~~dyed~~ died; ~~an~~ a
16. ~~are~~ is; ~~real~~ very
17. ~~play~~ played; ~~threw out~~ throughout
Synonym Watch: emphatic—forceful

Lesson 75
Answers may vary.
1. I haven't had any bites all day here.
2. I never catch anything in this part of the creek.
3. This fishing hole has never been a great spot for me.
4. However, Josh says he never fishes anywhere else.
5. I want to find a place where no one has fished before.
6. Josh says such places hardly exist anymore.
7. Let's not waste any more time at this fishing hole.
8. I haven't ever hiked up past the rapids.
9. A strenuous hike won't bother me.
10. The fishing up there can't be any worse than it is here.
Odd Word Out: The word *lasso* does not belong. The other four words could fit in the category "Fishing." *Lasso* could fit in the category "rodeo gear."

Lesson 77

PART I

1. <u>When Caroline stepped onto her new skateboard,</u> she felt very excited.
2. She had bought it <u>because her old one was not very good.</u>
3. <u>If she could jump the curb on the new board,</u> she would be happy.
4. <u>After she tried for an hour,</u> she was finally successful.

PART II

5. CX   6. (not complex)   7. CX

PART III

8. <u>that I saw on the fire escape this morning</u>
9. <u>who owns the delicatessen</u>
10. <u>which smells quite strong</u>

PART IV

11—13. Sentences will vary.

PART V

14. ~~he, went and~~   15. ~~like, and stuff~~   16. ~~there, it~~

Lesson 78

PART I

1. part-time
2. as soon as possible
3. good attitude
4. Experience preferred
5. No phone calls
6. equal opportunity employer
7. evenings a week

PART II

Answers will vary.
8. A salesclerk is needed from 5 P.M. to 9 P.M. three evenings a week, and from 9 A.M. to 6 P.M. on Saturday.

9. The salary is from $6 to $7 per hour.
10. The applicant should be familiar with bicycles.
11. The applicant should have a neat appearance and a good attitude.
12. A person should send a resume to Mr. Hughes at Box 1021, Austin, TX 73301.

Lesson 79

PART I

725 Princeton Ave.
Des Moines, IA 50309
February 16, 1998

Sales Manager
Mike's Music Store
P.O. Box 823
Des Moines, IA 50309

Dear Sales Manager:

I saw your advertisement for a sales assistant position in today's paper. I am very interested in the job. I have studied music since fourth grade, and I play piano, guitar, and drums. Could you please send me an application? I can also be reached at (515) 555-4011 if you would like to call me for an interview.

Yours truly,

Dana Hobbie

PART II

Dana Hobbie
725 Princeton Ave.
Des Moines, IA 50309

Sales Manager
Mike's Music Store
P.O. Box 823
Des Moines, IA 50309

Lesson 80
Answers will vary.

Lesson 81
Answers will vary.

Lesson 82
1. ~~thought; length~~
2. (c)
3. birds, city, cats, country, dogs, don't
4. (a) false
   (b) false
   (c) false
   (d) true

Lesson 83
1. compound
2. linking *or* being
3. independent *or* main; dependent
4. second *or* past
5. dependent
6. me; you; him; her; it; us; them (any three)
7. strong *or* sudden emotion
8. imperative

9. subject; verb
10. verb; subject
11. direct
12. -ing

13. antecedent
14. sentence
15. dependent clause

Lesson 84

PART I

1. known
2. Among
3. These
4. Its
5. Whose
6. There's
7. their
8. gone
9. Between
10. took
11. very
12. into
13. taken
14. into
15. knew
16. There
17. written
18. their
19. seen
20. there

PART II

Sentences will vary.

Lesson 85

PART I

lay, set, sat, lay, set, laid, laid, set, sitting, sitting, lying, laid, lay, set, lie, lying, sit, lie, lies, lay

PART II

Sentences will vary.

Lesson 86

PART I

1. accept   ac-cept
2. deposit   de-pos-it
3. envelope en-ve-lope
4. hundred   hun-dred
5. order   or-der
6. rather   rath-er
7. razor   ra-zor
8. thought   thought

PART II

9. having to do with the atmosphere or with aviation
10. apprise
11. vengeance
12. back
13. a seabird
14. mercans *or* mercari
15. the Greek goddess of victory
16. Answers will vary. Respellings should match those in the dictionary used.
17. skepticle
18. on land

Antonym Watch—insolent—ingratiating

Lesson 88

PART I

Letters will vary.

[student's own street address]
[student's city, state postal code, zip code]
[today's date]

Manager
Big Spin Bicycle Shop
1422 Bridge St.
Green Valley, AZ 85614

Dear Manager:

Please send me a catalog of the bicycles and equipment you have for sale. Thank you.

Sincerely yours,
[student's own name]

PART II

1. Whose   2. it's   3. taken   4. seen   5. gone

PART III

6. laid   7. sit   8. lie   9. Set   10. lying

Lesson 89

PART I

1. Great whales and dolphins are mammals and cetaceans. *simple*
2. They breathe air, and the females nurse their young with milk. *compound*
3. When they want to breathe, they must swim to the surface. *complex*
4. Isn't the blue whale the world's largest creature? *simple*
5. Although some cetaceans hunt large sea creatures, most eat small organisms. *complex*
6. Dolphins and porpoises look similar, but they are different. *compound*
7. The dolphin's greater size and intelligence set it apart. *simple*
8. Cetaceans often swim together and communicate with each other. *simple*
9. Usually when a dolphin gets sick, another dolphin helps it. *complex*
10. The sick dolphin rests, and the "nurse" helps it to the surface. *compound*
11. When a female cetacean gives birth, other females in the group usually help it. *complex*
12. Many dolphins and whales have large and complex brains. *simple*
13. Some scientists are studying dolphin communication. *simple*
14. Have any humans ever lived with dolphins? *simple*
15. Communication between people and dolphins may be possible. *simple*

PART II

Sentences will vary.

Lesson 90

1. received; direct object
2. had become; predicate noun
3. gave; indirect object
4. became; predicate noun
5. offered; direct object
6. spent; direct object
7. gave; indirect object
8. married; direct object
9. gave; indirect object
10. formed; direct object
11. was; predicate adjective
12. gave; indirect object
13. visited; direct object
14. was; predicate noun
15. Was; predicate noun

Connecting Meanings: auburn—reddish brown; augment—add to; audible—able to be heard. Sentences will vary.

Lesson 91

1. working; participle
2. Putting lids on cans of stew; gerund
3. to join the Amalgamated Meat Cutters Union; infinitive
4. to head her local; infinitive
5. rising fast; participle
6. Arguing for the rights of workers; gerund
7. determined; participle

8. <u>to open good jobs to women</u>; infinitive
9. <u>working as beef luggers or butchers</u>; gerund
10. <u>Serving as a union leader</u>; gerund
11. <u>to do well</u>; infinitive
12. <u>growing</u>; participle

PARTS II–IV

Answers will vary.

Lesson 92

PART I

1. <u>since people first sailed the seas</u>; adverb
2. <u>that reportedly has a monster</u>; adjective
3. <u>Because people love monster tales</u>; adverb
4. <u>who are fascinated by the legend</u>; adjective
5. <u>that proves the monster's existence</u>; adjective
6. <u>which is very deep</u>; adjective
7. <u>If clear pictures are ever taken</u>; adverb

PART II

Answers may vary.
8. Even though electronic equipment has given no indication of a monster's presence, some people believe in it.
9. Since I've never seen a clear picture of it, I don't believe in the monster.
10. Although many people have reported sightings of the monster, nobody has proved its existence.
11. While I was in Scotland, I stopped at Loch Ness to look for the monster.
12. Until I saw the thick fog, I didn't realize the foolishness of my plan.

Lesson 93

PART I

1. show	6. is	11. provide
2. lay	7. have	12. list
3. represent	8. are	13. identify
4. grows	9. is	14. does
5. fall	10. beats	

PART II

Sentences will vary.
Synonym Watch: flawed—imperfect

Lesson 94

PART I

Sentences will vary.
1. Clams and octopuses are mollusks.
2. Clams have a hard outer shell, but octopuses do not.
3. The body of an octopus is soft and boneless.
4. An octopus has two eyes and three hearts.

5. An octopus's gills are inside a cavity at the center of its body, and the octopus uses these gills to take oxygen from seawater.
6. The octopus draws water into its gills through its mantle cavity, and expels the water through a long tube called a funnel.
7. An octopus uses its eight arms and suckers to move across the sea floor.
8. A female octopus may lay as many as 100,000 eggs, but most of the young octopuses are devoured by predators.
9. Seals hunt and devour adult octopuses.
10. Other enemies of the octopus are large fish, toothed whales, and fishers.

PART II

Answers may vary.

compound subject: 1	compound predicate noun: 10
compound predicate: 6, 9	compound predicate adjective: 3
compound direct object: 4, 7	compound sentence: 2, 5, 8

Lesson 95

PART I

1. churches	8. lunches	15. watches
2. babies	9. cherries	16. radios
3. boxes	10. women	17. potatoes
4. witnesses	11. moose	18. sheep
5. children	12. excuses	19. pianos
6. valleys	13. men	20. heroes
7. shelves	14. pennies	

PART II

21. won't	25. they're	29. doesn't
22. you're	26. we'll	30. I've
23. isn't	27. hadn't	
24. I'm	28. he's	

PART III

31. the twins' friend	36. the town's mayor
32. our textbook	37. their prize
33. the family's cat	38. Jess's sled
34. the churches' bells	39. The brothers' dog
35. her ideas	40. Sanaz's cars

Lesson 96

1. don't	9. learn	17. learned
2. doesn't	10. sat	18. well
3. very	11. taught	19. good
4. any	12. you're	20. seen
5. made	13. in	21. Your
6. took	14. its	22. your
7. saw	15. well	23. You're
8. those	16. given	24. set

Lesson 97

916 North Aspen Street
Oklahoma City, OK 73106
July 10, 1998

Mrs. Tommie Webb
Skogsted Insurance Brokers
100 Sunrise Boulevard
Lawton, OK 73501

Dear Mrs. Webb:

On June 5, 1998, I wrote you asking how to purchase medical insurance. You sent me a pamphlet entitled "Protection and Peace of Mind." You also wrote that you would call me soon to arrange a meeting. I have heard nothing since then, and I have been unable to reach you by phone. If I don't hear from you by Friday, July 17, I will go elsewhere for my insurance.

Sincerely,

Felipe Alvarez

Word Whiz: inhabit, inhibit, inherit

Lesson 98

PART I

1. Although the meteorologist predicted rain, the sun is shining. *complex*
2. My best friend and my cousin play volleyball together often. *simple*
3. Volleyball is fun, but I prefer softball. *compound*
4. If you could star in any sport, which would you choose? *complex*

PART II

5. predicate noun
6. indirect object
7. predicate adjective
8. direct object

PART III

9. to order tempura; infinitive
10. Trying new foods; gerund
11. fried in batter; participle
12. to try sushi; infinitive

PART IV

13. that you have chosen; adjective
14. Although it is long; adverb
15. because it is so exciting; adverb
16. who wrote it; adjective

PART V

17. rides   18. are   19. perform   20. do

PART VI

Sentences will vary.

PART VII

29. crashes   31. waxes   33. women   35. deer
30. turkeys   32. cabbages   34. armies   36. tomatoes

PART VIII

37. the birds' chirps   39. the engineers' problem
38. their car   40. her hammer

INDEX OF TOPICS FEATURED IN LEVEL IV
(Numbers listed are page numbers.)